SILVER SCREEN
SACRED STORY

USING MULTIMEDIA IN WORSHIP

MICHAEL G. BAUSCH

FOREWORD BY DOUG ADAMS

AN ALBAN INSTITUTE PUBLICATION

Portions from chapter 2 appeared in the author's "Using Video Resources in the Worship Setting," a thesis-project submitted to the faculty of United Theological Seminary of the Twin Cities (New Brighton, Minn.: 1997), and in a series of articles appearing in *Church Worship: Resources for Innovative Worship* in April, May, and August of 1999.

Excerpts from *The Silents of God: Selected Issues and Documents in Silent American Film and Religion 1908–1925* by Terry Lindvall (Lanham, Md.: Scarecrow Press, 2001) are used by permission of the publisher. All rights reserved.

Scripture quotations, unless otherwise noted, are from the New Revised Standard Version of the Bible, copyright © 1989, Division of Christian Education of the National Council of the Churches of Christ in the United States of American and are used by permission.

Library of Congress Catalog Number 2002109032

ISBN 1-56699-271-0

CONTENTS

105072

Visual imagery is the primary language of our day and draws together people of all ages, races, genders, and classes. As people increasingly remember what they see more than what they hear, Michael Bausch's *Silver Screen, Sacred Story* helps us use this universal visual language to communicate the gospel through memorable worship and preaching to reach a wider public. He continues the reforming tradition encouraged by Martin Luther, who translated the Latin liturgy and Bible into German, and John Calvin, who translated liturgy and Scripture into French, to reach people in the sixteenth century who no longer knew Latin. Similarly in the mid-20th century, Vatican II led the Roman Catholic Church to translate worship into the language people speak in each land. Now, with visual image as the primary language, our task is to learn from Michael Bausch and others who translate worship into the language of the visual arts to communicate effectively to younger, visually oriented generations.

I believe that the importance of using visual arts in worship is about more than the language of worship, however. Just as Jesus used common bread and wine in the Last Supper, so we effectively sacramentalize the connection between worship and the world by using popular visual images in our preaching. I started incorporating the visual arts in worship 20 years ago by using only very fine films in worship. I quickly moved to more popular films, though, because a wider number of people were seeing them. Now I have come to see the value of using clips from TV shows as well as TV commercials.

For example, I met a professor of preaching from San Antonio who uses brief segments from Mexican TV soap operas, because that is what his people watch. I have used two chewing gum commercials to illustrate

Jesus' parable of the five wise and five foolish virgins. In the first commercial, a woman has waited so long to see a whale leap up from the sea that her chewing gum has lost it flavor. As she looks into her purse to find another stick of gum, the whale jumps up from the sea and then back into the water before she looks up. Having missed seeing the whale, which everyone else saw, the woman appears dejected at one end of the boat while others party at the other end. Similarly in the other gum commercial, an astronomer waits to see a comet he has been studying for years. As his gum loses flavor, he looks down to get another piece from his pocket; but the comet streaks by overhead before he looks up. He also misses what others see.

These TV commercials are memorable and brief—like Jesus' parables, and they can be used to remind us how God works. When we use film and video clips while they are in the theaters or are being shown on television, worshipers are reminded of that Sunday gathering and their relationship with God whenever they see references to those movies or watch TV the rest of the week.

Church historian Margaret Miles helps make the case for using visual imagery, rather than just words, for sacramental purpose. She details in *Image as Insight* (Beacon, 1985) how during earlier centuries the visual arts made the church more inclusive, but verbal communication made the church more exclusive. Today over 60 percent of our population, under age 60 and raised with television, remembers primarily by what is seen. Only 20 percent of the population, over age 60 and raised with radio, remembers primarily by what is heard. (The remaining 20 percent remembers kinesthetically, that is, by doing.) Churches having only verbal worship and preaching may as well use Latin, for the exclusively verbal mode no longer communicates with the vast majority of the population.

Not only has worshipers' primary language changed in the past several decades, but the visual arts themselves have changed. The visual arts had become increasingly abstract in modern times from the late 19th century until the 1960s, but in the past 40 years, historical and biblical subject matter have increasingly reappeared. So, one finds many more tacit and explicit references to Scripture in films and other arts these days. Bible scholar Northrup Frye called the Bible the great code of Western culture and explored how many figures in secular literature are subtle renderings of Jesus and other biblical characters. The Bible is also the great code for major motion pictures—*Dead Poets Society, Forrest*

Gump, countless episodes of *Star Wars, Saving Private Ryan,* and even *E.T.*—in which the main characters act in many ways like Jesus. (For further examples of the return of historical and biblical subject matter in every art form, see *Postmodern Worship and the Arts* [Resource Publications, 2002], which I co-edited with Michael Moynahan, and my earlier *Transcendence with the Human Body in Art: Segal, De Staebler, Johns, and Christo* [Crossroad, 1991].)

Michael Bausch has put into practice these and many other insights about the language and meaning of the visual arts in our culture. His suggestions throughout this book will be helpful whether a congregation plans to use a few film clips in a traditional Sunday morning sermon or develop a thoroughly visual Saturday evening worship service that functions much like a new church start. Bausch also offers plenty of inspiration for different ways to use visual images in worship. Worship planners can use this language to prepare memorable calls to worship, prayers of confession, and benedictions; to create brief videos of church retreats, work projects, and other missions to show during the announcements or the offertory; and in many other ways. Bausch details plans for a small church with little money or a large church with more extensive resources. He guides the beginner through the steps to make a sanctuary suitable for visual projections even when it cannot be darkened and whether one uses a TV monitor connected to a VHS or DVD playback system or a computer with digital projector.

Bausch also helpfully explores how films deal with theological themes and provides numerous examples of scriptural references in contemporary film and music. He discerns, for example, several biblical stories in *Spider-Man* and points out how baptismal imagery is significant in *O Brother, Where Art Thou.*

His pastoral suggestions are as valuable as his technological suggestions and theological observations. For example, he offers many ideas for ways gifted members can contribute to planning and implementation of a service based on visual arts. In the congregation he serves, film buffs provide him with videos or DVDs and with specific suggestions about which parts of films to use. Techies of all ages create and run the visual programs during worship. Film discussion groups help folks to deepen their insights into the relationship between film and faith.

All of these efforts lead to intergenerational appreciation and understanding of one another and the gospel message. Jesus instructed us to remember him when we break bread and drink wine wherever we are. Visual images, ubiquitous in our society, that have been tacitly and explicitly connected with the gospel, can also remind us of God's presence in our life wherever we are.

DOUG ADAMS
Professor of Christianity and the Arts
Pacific School of Religion
    and the Graduate Theological Union
Berkeley, California

You may have picked up this book because you are curious about the use of electronic media in worship. You have heard about screens, projectors, and computers, and have noticed articles and catalogs featuring the latest in worship technology. Maybe you are scrambling to catch up with the vision of your long-range planning committee and their thinking about doing something new to attract people to your church. Perhaps your worship committee has decided it is time to try something similar to what they are doing at a neighboring church. Some may be interested in developing a worship service that uses a different tone and style, and that incorporates the visual arts. It could be that you have already begun to use some worship technologies, and now you have $10,000 that someone gave you for technology that is still sitting in an account somewhere. Or, you are already building new facilities and the architects are saying you need to be wired for technology and should be thinking about adding screens to your space. Maybe you are already using some electronic media in worship and are beginning to understand that there is a lot more you could be doing with it.

This book grows out of several years of my own congregation's talking, thinking, and experimenting with multimedia worship, and several more years of actually providing a weekly multimedia worship experience. It also draws on the experiences of other churches and worship teams who are using media in their worship settings. What others and we have learned is that our sacred stories can be told with the help of the "silver screen." By combining the arts and theological reflection, ministry teams can discover new ways to do the work of the church: to worship God, to proclaim the Gospel, to join together as a multigenerational community of faith, and to work towards fulfilling the call to Abraham to be a blessing to "all the families of the earth" (Gen. 12:3), and the Great Commission, to "make disciples of all nations" (Matt. 28:19).

As more and more church people gain comfort with computer and projection technologies in their workplaces, schools, and homes, they are able to provide their churches with the technical knowledge and skills necessary to incorporate the appropriate equipment into the worship setting. With Bible study, theological reflection, and an ongoing discussion about the function and purpose of worship, lay and clergy teams can learn together how to use the power of audiovisuals to imaginatively and creatively communicate the Gospel.

During the course of this book, I will first take a look at some of the underlying issues associated with using multimedia in worship, provide examples of multimedia worship as developed in a variety of churches, and share some of the noticeable results. Next, I will describe a process for building acceptance for the use of visuals in your worship, and the importance of using one of many theoretical models for organizational change available to you. We will then explore how to use art, film, and contemporary music in the worship setting, and how to develop these media forms in ways that are faithful to the purposes of worship. Then we will look at the practical issues associated with producing multimedia worship, including the people resources needed, the planning process, the production guidelines you will want to consider, and the equipment you may need. An important part of this chapter is a discussion of U.S. copyright law, and how it relates to worship multimedia. The final chapters provide an annotated bibliography and a listing of Internet resources, a series of frequently asked questions (FAQs), and a Service of Dedication should you want to formally incorporate your projection screen into your sanctuary.

This book would not be possible were it not for the commitment to innovation that has been demonstrated by the Union-Congregational Church (UCC) of Waupun, Wisconsin, which helped envision, support, and grow the use of electronic multimedia as a part of weekly worship. For four years I have worked closely with an amazing team of persons from our church who have brought sustained creative energy to the planning, creative production, and leadership of our multimedia worship experiences. We have read scripture together, uncovered important themes, and learned how to talk theologically about music, film, and art. They have selected video clips, located visual illustrations, found songs, and artistically woven together sound and image to produce inspiring works of media art. Without the commitment and dedication of Teri Dary, Maggie Leu, Rich Dary, Mary Beatty, and Lisa Lenz, there would not have been a book to write.

What we have accomplished would not have been possible were it not for the vision of our "Towards 2000" working group. They had the foresight and creativity to look ahead to the turn of the millennium from their vantage point in the mid-1990s, and to wonder about how to develop worship experiences that would attract a new media generation. Nor would it have happened had it not been for the generous persistence of Tom and the late Margo Zerbel, who purchased our video-data projector and first computer, and Claudia and Will Waskow, who purchased a second-generation computer with DVD capabilities.

I am also grateful to John Jewell of the University of Dubuque Theological Seminary for asking me to serve as adjunct faculty in worship and media for their groundbreaking Certificate in Technology and Ministry program, and to my first group of students who brought such energy and dedication to learning how to use multimedia in worship. Eileen Crowley-Horak of Union Theological Seminary traveled from New York to study our multimedia worship services and interviewed our church members to learn about the impact of multimedia worship on their lives. Her work has affirmed our team's efforts and provided us fresh vocabulary for describing what they do.

My editor, Beth Ann Gaede, is quite skilled at helping her authors communicate as clearly as possible. She encourages logical thinking and clear writing. I have appreciated her gentle nudges, graceful assistance, and good humor, and I am grateful for all she has taught me as we have prepared this book. Whatever remains unclear is my responsibility, not hers!

I also owe great thanks to those seminarians at Pacific School of Religion who, three decades ago, believed in the power of multimedia to change lives and enliven the church: Michael Rhodes, Thom Tyson, Warren Mullen, Julius Young, Nels Gabbert, Stewart Hoover, and our teacher, George Conklin.

Finally, I thank my spouse, Catherine Ann Carlson, for her patience, support, listening ear, and thoughtful comments as I worked through the process of writing this book.

This work is not being offered to promote technology, but is provided, in the same spirit as J. S. Bach's famous dedication, "Soli Deo Gloria," to God alone be the glory.

CHAPTER 1

Multimedia and Worship

In 1910, a writer promoting the church's use of movies as part of "an effort for 'social justice'" asked Thomas Edison to write an editorial for a church periodical. Edison, whose experiments resulted in the modern motion picture in 1889, declared, "I believe that the motion picture presents a ready means in the hands of the broad minded, intelligent and informed workers for the world's good, for the innocent amusement, efficient instruction and the moral advance of the great masses of people."[1]

While some church leaders shared this optimism, there were others who raised the caution flag, seeing "Absolute danger in the Via Media—just another way of stepping into the current flowing away from God" and towards Satan.[2] Those who advocated the use of the new electrically powered moving picture technology as a tool of the church countered with this:

> The disfavor which is now meted out to the motion picture was aimed at the stereopticon a decade ago, at quartet singing several decades earlier, at the pipe organ before that, and still earlier at the Holy Bible printed in the vernacular; and yet, in God's own time every one of these religious agencies commended itself to the approval of the Christian people.[3]

Here we are, a century or more removed from that time, and we are still debating whether electronic multimedia can be used in authentic worship. One worship professor writes, "For churches whose primary role is the worship of God, they will find little use for (technology). Instead, they will surround their efforts with authentic spirituality which leans more toward creative endeavors than technological toys."[4] I once heard a seminary professor tell a clergy group that to use technology in worship is "wholesale capitulation to the values of media" that only the megachurches (i.e., big equals bad) could afford, support, and would dare to use. Another observer of today's worship scene says the big question worship leaders must decide is whether or not we want "machines" to "facilitate worship experiences."[5] Still others associate multimedia worship technologies with terms like "glitz," "trendy," "flash in the pan," "fluff," and "cream puff" theology. These critics seem to insist that the old nemesis "Via Media" must ever be quarantined to protect the church and its worship.

Such fears about technology are certainly not original. Every technological advance has faced suspicion and opposition. The 12th-century Latin Church saw the table fork as a "tool of the devil"[6] because of its association with wealth and Byzantine culture (which, incidentally, was highly iconographic). A 15th-century image depicting the printing press included skeletons lurking in the background, a warning against the danger of this new technology.[7] Some called for the banishment of the printing press even as others were finding it to be a brand new way to spread their ideas about the reformation of the church.[8] While many of today's critics write cautionary tales of the use of electronic technology in worship, I find them strangely silent about the printing press and other technologies once new to the church, but now widely accepted: duplicating machines, electric typewriters and word processors, amplified voice and music systems with wireless receivers, electronic pipe organs with memory chips and digital relay features, central heating systems with air conditioning, indoor plumbing, electric clocks, and unfermented grape juice (made possible by a technology that resulted from Pasteur's work during the time Edison was working on electricity and motion picture equipment).[9]

We who plan and lead worship live in a "both/and" world. Our world includes the rich stories, narratives, and themes of our religious faith. We also live in a world that includes the silver screens through which we view TV, video, and movies. In worship, we proclaim the stories of faith and we use a variety of communication devices to tell them: spoken and written words; music that is seen, sung, and heard; and visual arts of architecture, stained glass, fabric art, sculpture, poster, and painting. Unfortunately, much of the worship debate takes an "either/or" approach that promotes one technology or medium over another as the best way. Multimedia technology is one of life's realities, and while these media are ever changing, they are here to stay. While some may think of multimedia in worship as an "either you use it or you do not" proposition, I think it more helpful to think of it as a "both/and" opportunity. Authentic worship may include both word and image, oral liturgy and multimedia visual arts (as well as music and silence, movement and sitting, and so on).

Theologians like Paul Tillich, and more recently, Sally McFague, have described an approach to life and faith that is simultaneously an embrace and a judgment. McFague says that every theology must have its Catholic side and its Protestant side, "the 'Catholic' sacramental appreciation of the world joined with the 'Protestant' prophetic witness to divine transcendence."[10] We embrace the substance of the world, including the productivity, creativity, and technological progress of our culture, as a gift from God, and we maintain the principle of a critical distance from culture through the word of prophetic judgment. We live with this paradox continually when we understand and know God in both the incarnation and the resurrection, in immanence and transcendence. Multimedia technologies may at times be embraced, and at other times resisted.

A Tower of Babel and an Ark of Salvation

Genesis gives us a "both/and" example about technology, teaching how at times we must distance ourselves from it, and at other times we must embrace it. The story of the building of the Tower of Babel is an example of people using technical skill to call attention to themselves and their abilities, rather than to the glory of God. They sought to make a name for themselves and use their skills to build a tower into the heavens. God declared this to be a wrong use of technology, and confused the languages of the people so they could not communicate and fulfill their sinful purpose. Contrast this story with another story out of the same book. The story of Noah's ark is about using technical skill for God's purpose. It is God who gives Noah the technical specifications (three decks of gopher wood and pitch with a roof and door, 300 x 50 x 30 cubits), and says, "Make it." The ark, of God's design and built by human hands, becomes an instrument of God's saving power.

These simple stories can offer the help we need as we consider using technology in worship. We both embrace and maintain a critical distance. We consciously use our technical skill and equipment to serve God's saving power at work in the world.

The Mother Tongue of Electronic Multimedia

I write this book from my perspective as a parish pastor who has grown up in both the church and in a media-saturated culture. I am a child of the church. It was in church where I found a sense of belonging, where Sunday school teachers, other parents, and the grandparents of the congregation affirmed me, encouraged me, and blessed me. I am a child of media culture too. I listened to the radio on my grandpa's knee before we had a TV, and remember the day my father brought our first TV into our house. We went to the movies to see Disney films. I listened to love songs of the early '60s as well as the protest music that paralleled our country's deeper involvement in Vietnam. Our music was reflecting our experience and bringing new experiences to us. It was shaping us. TV was shaping us too . . . bringing us the Vietnam War, bringing us pictures of how African Americans were treated in the south, bringing us the assassinations, bringing us advertisements that promoted a way of life.

Through my high school, college, and seminary years, I saw how the movies and music of my generation were artistic expressions that reflected and shaped our culture and world. Those who taught me understood the inescapable relationship between faith and ordinary life, suggesting reading the newspaper in one hand and the Bible in the other. We youth of the church who were coming of age in a world of TV, movies, and the social protest music of the '60s interpreted the movies we watched and the music we listened to through our understanding of biblical faith. Films such as *The Sandpiper* (1965), *Cool Hand Luke* (1967), and *Guess Who's Coming to Dinner* (1967) addressed social and theological issues. Songs like "7 O'Clock News/Silent Night" and "The Sound of Silence" by Simon and Garfunkel, "We Gotta Get Out of This Place" by the Animals, "Let's Live for Today" by the Grass Roots, and "Eleanor Rigby" by the Beatles also confronted theological issues. Some of the folk-protest songs of the Vietnam and Civil Rights era by artists like Phil Ochs, Bob Dylan, Joan Baez, and Marvin Gaye stimulated discussions about faith and social conscience. Just as Jesus dramatized lessons about God's reign by telling stories from everyday life, we learned that the stories found in popular movies and music could also serve as parables of life that contained lessons about the reign of God.

At the same time, we were also learning of another side to the mass media, and its promotion of consumerism through advertising, its negative portrayals of women and racial minorities, and its contribution to escalating societal violence with its graphic, violent content. Then, as now, children and teens were giving more hours to TV than to school and reading, and were exposed to thousands of commercials. Groups like the American Academy of Pediatrics grew concerned that children were being exposed to sexism, violence, and sexual behavior through the mass media, and recommended that parents restrict the amount of time their children spent in front of the TV. We also learned that it was possible to "talk back" to the TV and oppose its negative influences. The National Council of Churches developed its "Television Awareness Training"[11] with that purpose in mind. Children, youth, and adults within the church could become active users of mass media by learning to identify the values that were being promoted through their media, and to compare and contrast them with their religious values. We who worked in youth and educational ministries labored in the hope that by encouraging active involvement in a media-critical process, we could help develop persons who would hold fast to religious values while opposing the dominant values of an increasingly violent and consumerist culture.

Catholic practical theologians assisted in this work by making distinctions between "mass media" and "group media,"[12] noting how the power of multimedia could be harnessed by church people for the purposes of promoting the Gospel. People could be trained to use readily available media technologies (or group media) such as 8 mm film, portable videotape equipment, and 35 mm slides to fashion messages promoting Gospel values such as peace, love, and justice. Twenty-five years ago, Catholic theologians called electronic media a new language and said my generation was "the first audiovisual generation" because "the new language is for them a continuous experience from the very first day of their existence. It is their mother tongue."[13] All of us born since World War II have been "licked into shape" by this mother tongue.[14] We have grown up multilingual, understanding the many tongues of communication media. We are comfortable with oral language, having learned to listen and speak. We are comfortable with print media, having been taught to read and write. We are comfortable with electronic language, having learned to watch TV, view films, and listen to a wide range of music.

During the 1960s and '70s, many churches invested in the group media, affordable audiovisual equipment, for use in their educational ministries. Pastors and teachers used a variety of visual technologies to gain and hold the attention of their learners, and to help them understand their lessons.

They displayed posters, prints, and Bible maps, wrote words on newsprint, drew diagrams on chalkboards, and affixed figures to felt boards. They showed transparencies, filmstrips, slides, movies, and other printed material through the use of overhead projectors, filmstrip projectors, slide projectors, movie projectors, and opaque projectors. Before the advent of today's media technologies, it took a fair amount of time and effort to assemble the material that was to be projected, find the proper projector, get an extension cord, check the bulb, locate the screen, and set it all up. Because of these necessary steps, it was easier to keep the equipment in the classrooms, but sometimes a worship leader would wheel a projector into the sanctuary to show some song lyrics (often without copyright permission) on an overhead projector, or a filmstrip or 35 mm slides of religious art. In the case of film, it was virtually impossible in those days to show a movie scene because the movies were hard to find and they were very expensive to rent. It was also a nuisance trying to figure out how to thread the film into the heavy old 16 mm projectors without breaking it on the metal sprockets, find the single scene we wanted to show, hope that the projector bulb was not burned out, and pray that the old projector did not freeze up and melt the film by the heat of the lamp. Today's technologies, however, make it much easier for worship leaders to use multimedia in worship sanctuaries.

New Technologies and New Possibilities

While electronic multimedia have been used in churches for a long time, today's equipment is lighter, portable, and simpler to use. Recent technological advances with the personal computer make it very easy to store words and images on a single computer, and to display them on a screen with a single projector, rather than using a number of different specialized projectors. Personal computers can be used to store and organize thousands of slides, photographs, movies, maps, diagrams, and filmstrips. A lightweight projector can be connected to a computer to display everything stored in it: pictures that have been scanned into the computer's hard drive, photographs taken with digital cameras, video sequences taped with a camera or captured from an existing tape or disc, images legally copied from the internet, and 35 mm slides that have been scanned into the computer. Such digitized images can be easily stored, labeled, organized, accessed, and displayed without requiring all of the steps of the old systems. Someone with a personal slide collection no longer needs to sort the slides on slide tables, insert them upside down into a carousel, and face them in the right direction. Once in a computer, the picture can be copied into a software program and displayed, appearing to the viewer just like an old-fashioned slide show. With certain software, however, a person may add words, animations, sounds, and a number of other features that the older slide technology could not provide.

What is also different in today's world is the broad range of technologies covered by the umbrella term *multimedia*. Those who like concise definitions could consult the 235 pages of terms and acronyms listed in *The Dictionary of Multimedia*. The book's general definition of *multimedia* is "interactive digital media," arising out of "a synthesis of traditional forms of art and communication with rapidly evolving fields of computing and networking."[15] The term *multimedia* is now a broad horizontal term that covers a number of disciplines, including audio, graphics, hardware, networking, software, telecommunications, and video. The inherent complexity in all of this "requires teamwork and the contribution of many minds and hands."[16] Using today's multimedia in worship is "an art, a science, and a new medium of expression"[17] which requires the creative and collaborative efforts of a large number of people within a congregation.

Today's technology allows us to connect a tiny laptop computer to a small projector and show a movie, words, or pictures on a light-colored surface as small as your smallest slide screens or as big as your largest wall. This makes it easy to include audio and visual illustrations in the classroom, and in the worship setting.

Authentic Change

While new technologies may make it more convenient to use electronic media in worship, congregational practice or tradition may not welcome them into the sanctuary.

A pastor or worship committee in touch with a congregation and knowledgeable about the realities of parish ministry knows that bringing such technology into the worship setting is a change that will concern some people. As long as this change fits the core values of a congregation and flows out of a congregation's historical sense of purpose and mission, the change will be less jarring. The changes that people perceive to be peripheral to the mission and purpose of their church are the changes they will most resist. Technology that is seen as just another expensive furnishing in a church, or as a source of theological friction, is technology that is disconnected from the heart and soul of a church. Unless multimedia technologies are linked to the core values of a congregation and church's sense of mission and purpose, they will be seen as an undesired change.

In the book, *Good to Great*, management consultant Jim Collins and his team interviewed hundreds of executives to try to uncover the characteristics that commonly appear in thriving, long-standing companies and organizations.[18] They were surprised to find that 80 percent of the executives they interviewed did not mention technology as one of the top factors in their companies' transformation from good to great. This led Collins to conclude, "We find that technology is an accelerator of greatness already in place."[19] Using multimedia technologies in worship, by itself, will not bring greatness to your church, but it can accelerate the greatness you already have going in worship, education, mission, and community building.

Adding a screen, projector, computer, and visuals to worship is a change for a congregation that can be experienced as being part of the central mission and purpose of a church: to effectively communicate the Word of God. When carefully related to the mission of the church, the creative energies of a committed group of laity, and the best preaching and pastoral sensitivities of a worship leader, worship technologies can be servants of the Holy Spirit's work of transforming lives. This is why so many churches have easily added screens to their sanctuaries, because it is clear to the congregation that the technology contributes to the communication of the Word. They understand that visuals, like words, can feed and nourish souls.

Adding multimedia audiovisuals can also assist in the transformation of souls. Walter Brueggemann believes "the purpose of preaching and worship is transformation."[20] He defines this transformation as "the slow, steady process of inviting each other into a counterstory about God, world, neighbor, and self."[21] This transformation is accomplished through liturgy and proclamation that recognize "people in fact change by the offer of new models, images, and pictures of how the pieces of life fit together—models, images and pictures that characteristically have the particularity of narrative to carry them."[22] The narrative of worship is the story of faith as found in scripture, and interpreted by tradition and the gathered community today. Each time we gather to worship, we are asked to experience the narrative once again by means of everything worship leaders use to communicate the story that day. Media technologies offer yet another tool to "tell the old, old story."

Those wary about technology in worship seem to be most concerned that God, not the technology, be served in our worship, that any technology be used in worship with a sense of responsibility and humility. These concerns come out of the Protestant word of prophetic judgment and critique. The worshiping community and its leadership must continually evaluate all uses of multimedia in worship. This is accomplished by regular discussion about the role and function of worship in their lives, and about how multimedia technology can be a creative tool for viewing God's story through the lens of our own story, and reflecting on our story by the light of God's story.

Multimedia Preaching and Liturgy

Preachers have been taught to season their sermons with stories, anecdotes, and illustrations in order to gain and hold the attention of their listeners. A simple parable from daily life, when told in a faith context ("the kingdom of God is like . . .") not only illustrates a message, but also is the message. Those who preach regularly have learned that using these references to everyday life quickly captures attention. These illustrations emerge out of personal experiences and from what is gleaned from media such as newspapers, comic strips, books, magazines, TV programs, novels, plays, movies, and popular music.

With the advent of affordable and powerful computer and projector technology, it is possible to project these materials upon a screen in the worship sanctuary. During a sermon it is possible to display the sermon outline, as well as colorful charts, maps, photographs, paintings, sculptures, scripture references, or a short segment from a popular movie. Besides the sermon, other parts of the worship service can also be visually enhanced with displays of words to hymns, prayers, and announcements, as well as pictures to serve as a backdrop to the words or to illustrate an announcement, photographs of members, and dramatic footage of mission outreach programs.

Our parish nurse suggested we address the theme of organ and tissue donation during worship. At our traditional worship service, our nurse commented about the organs and tissues that people can donate. While she spoke, we showed a drawing of a human body that identified the various organs that can be donated. As she explained that on the back of every driver's license was an anatomical gift statement the individual could sign, we displayed a photograph of that section of the drivers' license. We also displayed a copy of the organ donor sticker that could be affixed to the front of the license, and a picture of a donor card that was available for people to take home. These simple pictures helped people understand the nurse's message, and showed them what they could sign to become a donor.

At another one of our services, which uses media more extensively, we showed the same visuals and added a video clip. We showed a scene from the film *Return to Me* (2000), a story based on the experience of two families and how a heart transplant brought them together. The three-minute scene we showed was a montage within the film showing the grieving husband who had authorized his wife's heart to be transplanted, another family praying that their daughter receive a heart, the heart being transported to the operating room, and the young woman breathing on her own after receiving the transplanted heart. At the conclusion of this film clip, one of our members spoke to the congregation of how her father had received a donor heart that gave him another three years of life. As she spoke, we displayed one picture on the screen: a copy of the newspaper obituary of the young man whose heart was donated to her father. The visuals stimulated understanding and response. People in the sanctuary reported they were emotionally moved by the film clip, by the testimony of the woman who spoke so movingly of her family's experience with organ donation, and the words projected on the screen telling of another family who decided to donate their son's heart after his death in a motorcycle accident. We communicated a clear and powerful message by combining visuals with an oral presentation.

On Memorial Day weekend a pastor went to the local cemetery with a digital camera, took photographs of various gravestones, monuments, trees, flowers, and a pond, and assembled them into a short program that was displayed while the Beatles' song, "In My Life" played in the background. This set the stage for the sermon about the importance of remembering. Another pastor selected a three-minute sequence from a denominational mission video and showed it during the offertory to vividly illustrate what that congregation's support did to accomplish a specific mission project. A sixth-grade Sunday school class invited children in the lower grades to draw pictures of things and people for which they were thankful, scanned the pictures into a computer, and displayed them on a screen while a song about generosity played on the stereo.

As more people experience this power, they begin to wonder how to use visual equipment to project words, photographs, and video on their screens. In the National Congregations Study of 1998, only 12 percent of congregations reported using visual projection equipment in their most recent service.[23] I would guess this figure is much higher today, based on the increasing interest in learning about using such equipment. A company specializing in selling and installing projection equipment in church sanctuaries reported in 2002 that they had received inquiries from 100,000 churches over a 10-year period of time.[24] A growing number of churches are investigating using visual equipment to project words, photographs, and video on their screens.[25]

- A Presbyterian church in Oregon rented an 8 ft. x 8 ft. screen and projected words to their worship hymns, and displayed pictures to accompany a choral introit.
- A United Methodist church in Wisconsin installed a ceiling-mounted screen to display the words to their responsive and unison prayers during a contemporary service.
- A Reformed church in South Dakota uses denominational video clips to help promote the missions they support.
- A UCC minister in Illinois adds a video clip of a recent film to make a point during the sermon.
- A Roman Catholic church in Ohio produces short audiovisual presentations that are shown following communion, giving people the chance to meditate while listening to the music and seeing the visuals.
- A Disciples of Christ church in Iowa borrowed equipment so the youth group could display pictures to illustrate the music they selected from CDs.
- A Presbyterian pastor in Kansas videotaped an interview with a long-time member confined to a nursing home, and "brought her to church" by showing an excerpt from the tape during the "joys and concerns" time before the pastoral prayer.
- A UCC congregation in Arizona blends jazz music, dance, and visual presentations to invite people to communion.

As these churches have found, there are opportunities to use visual communication within the structure of even the most traditional worship.

These churches have found ways to show an announcement, project words of hymns, illustrate a sermon, or stimulate awareness of a special project. Here are some more examples of ways electronic media can be used to enhance a worship service.

Announcements

- Type bulletin announcements into slides and display them on a screen.
- Take pictures with a digital camera, or scan into a computer photos from other sources to illustrate the announcement or to show people and places of interest to the church.
- Show a short (one to two minutes) video clip of a recent project or event at church.
- Show pictures of new members, church leaders, church school teachers, newborns, and homebound members.
- Display music, art, video, or special production credits. These can be projected on a screen as people gather for worship and listen to the prelude.
- Post questions about Bible trivia or congregational trivia, with answers following.
- Stimulate people's awareness of the worship theme by showing a relevant video clip.
- Prepare the congregation for the sermon by displaying the scripture text for the day. The sermon points and theme could be shown too.

Calls to Worship and Responsive Prayers

- Display words to prayers on the screen, giving people a chance to look upward while reading the prayers.
- Select a short film clip (one to two minutes) that relates to the worship theme and can serve as an introduction to the worship service.

Hymns, Choruses, and Other Music

With proper copyright permission, these can be displayed on the screen so people look up as they sing.

- Pictures related to the lyrics can be displayed alongside the lyrics or behind them. Light-colored fonts are easily seen against darker backgrounds.

- When worship features a solo or duet as part of a service, display pictures that fit the theme of the music. For example, one church played a CD of the song "Ave Maria" at Christmas and displayed a variety of religious artworks depicting Mary and Jesus. Religious art, drawings from the church school, photography, and video clips can be pieced together into a slide program and accompanied by prerecorded music or by vocal or instrumental music from church members.

Scripture

- Display the scripture passage on the screen or show a picture representing the main idea of the passage.
- Introduce a scripture reading by showing a scene from Bible movies that shows the story you are featuring.

Offertory

- Introduce your offering period by showing a short video of a mission project your church supports.
- Show pictures of church people and staff involved in various church ministries and activities as the offering is received.

Sermon

- Display the key texts and points you want people to remember in the sermon.
- Use words, symbols, a photograph, or a work of art to anchor a sermon point.
- Show a short video clip (two to three minutes) to introduce the sermon or to illustrate a point during the sermon.
- Use music, still pictures, and video productions to creatively supplement and enhance the sermon.

Prayers

- Display pictures of persons or situations for which you are asking prayers.

Benediction

- Display properly permitted lyrics to a closing benediction song or show a picture that encapsulates the theme of the worship.

Postlude

- Display music, art, video, and production credits on screen as people leave.

Special Services

- Some churches use visuals during special worship services as an opportunity to call attention to the occasion or the people being recognized. When Armistice Day (November 11) fell on a Sunday, one pastor had her military veterans submit photographs from their service days and they were scanned into a computer and projected on a screen during a special ceremony honoring the veterans in the church.
- As churches assembled in prayer after the events of September 11, 2001, some put together images from the tragedy with musical accompaniment. They selected photographs that depicted various scenes of grief, people coming together to comfort one another, and expressions of hope. Some churches took this as an occasion to rekindle patriotism, while others found imagery to remind members of their relationship to the global community.
- Confirmation Sunday and services honoring graduates are opportunities to gather photographs of the youth when they were infants and toddlers, and display them with their most recent picture. Some churches have found parents willing to assemble these visual programs and select the soundtrack, a song or piece of music that can be sung or played while the slides are shown on the screen.
- Stewardship Sunday provides another opportunity for visual enhancements. Church school children and their teachers have taken photographs of various church staff and programs and put them into a program showing the ministries of the church. Ask the children to draw or color pictures of the church facilities, programs, and people, and scan them into a computer for insertion into a slide program. Add slides with additional written information such as your church's giving statistics, budget allocations, and perhaps a scripture reference and

show the entire program during the offertory or during a stewardship moment.

- Sermon series about biblical places and events are opportunities for visual illustrations. To accompany a sermon series on the missionary journeys of Paul, for example, show pictures of the places where Paul went as they appear today. Use maps to illustrate the routes he took. Display scripture passages with the pictures serving as a background. Supplement the sermon points with these images. Quietly play an audiotape of sounds of the sea or nature to accompany the message, helping transport the congregation to Paul's time and place. Show short video scenes of films which feature Paul's journeys or which illustrate an experience he may have had before or during the sermon.

The Buzz from Pulpit and Pew

As you can see from the examples, there is no one way to use multimedia in worship. Those who have tried it have found that it enlivens the worship experience of the congregation. As part of a seminary project, a group of pastors experimented with using multimedia in their worship settings. Their comments demonstrate a growing excitement about ways that multimedia can contribute to exciting worship services.[26]

- I have learned that the Lord is able to perform miracles with an outdated laptop and a borrowed projector to touch the hearts of his people. I have learned that pictures added to the words of a song can minister much more effectively than words alone.
- I have learned that laypersons can get pretty excited about coming alongside of the pastor to put together a service with multimedia. I have learned that you can make some folks in the church pretty scared about the introduction of a new worship service because it may make the church seem tacky or draw the wrong people.
- People love worship that opens them to experience God. When they know something is going to happen they come expectantly. Using pictures to enhance a psalm or a song or including movie clips in the sermon makes them more open to the possibility of something happening. I had wondered if the media would distract or overwhelm the worship. But I have found that the media enhances the worship.
- I am learning a lot about theology in movies. If the writers went to so much trouble to put it in there in the first place, then we owe it to

ourselves and our congregations to pull it back out and point it out. If we can do this we will all learn a lot more about theology in everyday life.

- It really is true that you cannot lead worship—preach and run all the equipment and have a smooth flowing service. Letting others help with planning and execution really does make life much less stressful.
- I learned through these past few months that media enhanced worship must be a team approach. It takes more and longer-range planning than what most of us would call traditional worship. It involves more people out of necessity.
- The technology is one good reason for a team approach. Another is that other people have great ideas that would have never occurred to me.
- Truly involving laypeople in the worship planning process has been refreshing because I hear different ideas and understandings of scriptures I have worked with for years.

What are some of the results of multimedia worship? Different pastors report:[27]

- We have discovered that using the projector and computer enhances our worship. Our services are now filled with young families, rows of teens, and clusters of college students. All who attend are clearly growing in their faith, and they are inviting others to join them in this exciting journey.
- Attendance has risen by 50 people or more than 40 percent. Of those who are new to us, approximately 80 percent are classically "unchurched."
- Almost immediately I noticed more men in the congregation. These were men who refused to come to church for years in the old building, but were drawn to the multimedia. They commented that the church had finally entered the new age and was therefore more relevant to them.
- Response has been overwhelmingly positive, with a few quiet grumbles.

The congregation I serve provides a weekly media-intensive worship service in addition to a traditional service and an informal worship service (three morning services). The media-intensive worship service is organized around a scriptural theme. Four to five media are selected for their relevance to the theme: video clips, music from popular culture (including songs the children, youth, and adults hear on their radios and CDs), and photography or art selected to illustrate the music. Below are comments from some who have worshiped in this style of service explaining how they understand what happens.[28]

- Adding media to worship makes it more compelling. There never seems to be a shortage of songs and film clips in which to find some spiritual or universal meaning.
- We don't have to "pull teeth" to get my 16-year-old son to come.
- It's fun with music and videos that blend with the sermon.
- It gets my energy rising for the rest of the day and gets me thinking about God.
- I'm in that age where you're so used to media that we appreciate the media, and this service drives home the message in a way that we haven't had in any other worship experiences.
- It's not just about a movie clip or the newest Dixie Chicks song. It's how the media is woven together to create or bring out the scripture message.

My own experience with this service confirms what other pastors have reported. We have attracted more men. We have attracted younger people, especially those born since 1960, but by no means does this mean only younger people can relate to the media. We have grandparents who accompany their children and grandchildren to our worship services. We have attracted inactive members because the worship service speaks their "mother tongue" of multimedia language. Those who spend more time with music, video, computer imagery, and film than they do with books enjoy the way our media service pulls out religious content from cultural material. Those who attend the service invite friends and relatives who are bored with what they call wordy, repetitive worship.

Another group excited about this style of worship is the group of volunteers who plan, produce, and present the media-intensive worship service. Church members prepare imagery to accompany music that illustrates a worship theme. Other volunteers who are familiar with computer technologies prepare slides, scan photos, or edit video. Others assist with wiring and rewiring equipment as needed or researching additional equipment that the church might need in the future. Children, youth, and adults work together to suggest music and film clips they think our planning team could incorporate into worship. The planning team has become good at teaching others how to use computer software, the Internet, scanning equipment, and digital cameras. Those who learn the new skills are then invited into providing media art that combines sound and visuals to illustrate a scripture or worship theme. Developing multimedia worship has revitalized an existing congregation, and has started a buzz that causes members to invite others into the church and incorporate these new ones into the life and work of the congregation.

Just Sitting There?

Even as many churches are discovering the communication power of multimedia in worship services, there are those who worry that there is something wrong about using multimedia technologies in worship. "The true nature of worship is to engage a participatory congregation in a God directed response of praise and thanksgiving for the Missio Dei; the mission of God to rescue the world through Jesus Christ," writes one worship professor.[29] He then accuses those who use electronic technology in worship of jeopardizing such participation by putting on a "show." Marva Dawn, whose *Reaching Out without Dumbing Down* is a favorite among those deeply suspicious of using visual technologies in worship, quotes Douglas Webster on the danger of "transforming a congregation into an audience, transforming proclamation into performance or transforming worship into entertainment."[30] The underlying assumptions of these critics are that (1) adding projected visuals to worship encourages passivity as people sit and watch and (2) traditional, wordy worship, during which people sit and listen, somehow is not passive. What makes listening more participatory than watching? In fact, sitting and listening is what most people do in worship.

In *How Do We Worship?*, Mark Chaves reports findings about worship in the United States from the 1998 National Congregations Study. "Empirically," he writes, "producing worship in the United States means getting people together to sing and listen to somebody talk."[31] Most of us who plan and produce worship presume that people are always processing the information they receive during a worship service. Worship leaders trust that the printed prayers and preached sermon will have an effect on worshipers' hearts and minds. When a preacher preaches to us, we may sit and daydream, we may allow ourselves to go with the flow of the message to see where it will take us, or we may emotionally and intellectually interact with the content. The worship leader may not see evidence of this internal process, but trusts that it happens. Is not the same process at work when a person watches something? Can we learn to trust that people are able to creatively interact with technologically mediated imagery they might watch or experience during a worship service? Instead of calling worshipers "passive," media theorists are trusting that internal processes are at work as people "take in" multimedia, and they are calling those people a "creative audience."[32] They understand that the people are thinking and responding even as they sit silently experiencing the words, music, and pictures of worship. The creative audience is a group that experiences the media art and is actively changed and transformed by the experience. Continually being shaped by media, group members are also reshaping it and adapting it freely and consciously into their own meaning systems. The audience is always reacting and responding to what they see and hear and, as in a traditional worship experience, formulating its own thoughts and opinions about the relationship of the message to their own lives. To presume passivity because someone is watching, and to presume activity when someone listens, proves nothing but a bias towards oral-print arts and against the visual-electronic arts.

Delighting the Heart and Mind

The church communicates to God, about God, with God, and for God by its worship, education, discipleship, and mission. Through the sharing of the Gospel in story, song, word, and picture, hearts are opened, minds are changed, and lives joined together in a blessed harmony.

A verse of the hymn "For the Beauty of the Earth" lyrically proclaims that what we see and what we hear can remind us that we live in the world as people created with sensory equipment. When our sensory experience takes us deep into our hearts and minds, we praise God for the delightful experience of a "mystic harmony."

For the joy of ear and eye,
For the heart and mind's delight,
For the mystic harmony
Linking sense with sound and sight,
Lord of all to thee we raise
This our hymn of grateful praise.[33]

There is joy in ear and eye, delight in heart and mind, and from this audio and visual harmony, God can lead us to new life in the world. In the following pages, I tell the story of how we can use multimedia technology and be faithful and authentic in our worship.

CHAPTER 2

Strategies for Developing Support

In a pamphlet written for the South Congregational Church of New Britain, Connecticut, the Rev. Herbert Jump described for his congregation what he called, "A Motion Picture Service of Worship," and recommended:

> Let the hymns and prayers be as usual. Let the Scripture lesson be illustrated with a film exhibiting the very incident narrated by the Bible. Let the sermon be on a practical topic like temperance, honesty, loyalty, prayer, the purity of the home pluck or self-sacrifice, and let the sermon be illuminated by two "motion picture parables" from present-day life.[1]

What amazes me is that he and his church were discussing using film in worship in the year 1910. Jump and other preachers writing around the same time used words like *vigor*, *vividness*, and *eloquence* to describe how preaching with moving pictures would bring a lively, engaging message into their worship services. Ninety-two years later, I can report that after four years of offering a motion picture worship service, the Rev. Jump is correct. The vigor and vividness of adding visuals to our worship has drawn the largest attendance of our three morning services, attracted new members, enlisted the gifts of a wide array of people, generated new financial support, and revitalized our worship. During this time period, we have used nearly 250 popular songs, accompanied them with thousands of images of people, nature, and artworks, and have shown 210 video clips from recent films.

None of these things happened overnight, of course. We did not show up one Sunday and say, "today we are going to have a multimedia worship experience." Adding multimedia audio and visuals to our worship took a number of years of careful introduction, experimentation, and evaluation.

It may be that in today's world of greater acceptance of computers, screens, and projectors, and in churches more open to experiment and change, some congregations may be able to introduce multimedia more quickly and less gradually. The purpose of this chapter is to share with you the gradual, momentum-building process that the congregation I serve experienced as they moved from using very little visual art in worship to incorporating a screen, projector, and a full array of audiovisual material.

In the book *Good to Great*, Jim Collins, a management research consultant, tells of his study of companies who incorporated significant changes into their business. He and his research team report that the companies who made the leap from being just good companies to great companies initiated a series of incremental, gradual steps, one after the other. These steps built a momentum within the organization that eventually led to a breakthrough to significant growth. Calling this process the "Flywheel Effect,"[2] Collins has us imagine the task of pushing a large metal disk (a flywheel) that is resting on an axle. Because of the weight of the disk, it will take many small pushes to get it moving. After many, many small pushes, the point of breakthrough is reached when the accelerating momentum of the disk now works with you and for you. You do not have to push as hard, since the increasing velocity of the heavy disk has made it easier to push. Collins found that the companies and organizations that worked towards their goal incrementally found the greatest success. I like this analogy because it fits what happened within my own congregation as we gradually pushed for incorporating visual arts into our worship.

Small Efforts and Big Progress

All churches have already incorporated visual arts into their worship spaces. The architecture of the space includes visual symbols and cues such as clusters of grapes carved into wooden frames, Greek symbols on banners and paraments, stories in stained-glass windows, and the shape of the worship space itself. Long naves, raised altars, and the positioning of lecterns, pulpits, communion tables, and baptismal fonts all represent meanings determined by architects and worship committees, who were content to make use of familiar, traditional forms and symbols. Printed bulletin covers offer visual support to a worship theme. Many clergy have included sermon outlines and quotations in the printed order of worship, or have added bulletin inserts featuring mission messages and other announcements supported by photography and art. Most modern preachers have offered children's sermons and given object lessons with bookmarks, coins, plants, weights, dinnerware, ropes, and bags filled with similar objects. Some preachers have used objects in the course of their sermons, including bicycles, yokes, knapsacks, staffs, and costumes. Some have brought newsprint pads and chalkboards to the pulpit area to write words or draw simple pictures to help with the sermon presentation. Still others have posted maps of biblical geography or have displayed easels containing a religious painting or print.

Worshipers are comfortable with, and maybe even expect to see, such visual elements in a worship setting. They expect an even wider array of visual media in educational settings. In fact, most churches have been using multimedia in their educational settings for generations. A tour of your church's closets will reveal filmstrip projectors, slide projectors, 16 mm film projectors, overhead and opaque projectors, videotape machines, posters, filmstrips, slide programs, videotapes and films, and a full array of art supplies. To bring some of these media from the classrooms into the worship sanctuary is possible with a few pushes on the flywheel, and a matter of gradually building a climate of acceptance.

Opening Minds and Hearts

Before starting to use visual arts in the worship of the church I serve, they had been used in four areas of church life: the church school, youth retreats, premarital counseling, and occasional adult education programs.

Church School

Many churches use curricula that include art to supplement and illustrate the lessons. My own congregation is fortunate to include some art teachers and artists, and one year we asked them to develop a visual art program designed to supplement the lectionary-based church school lesson. They were asked to bring to the church school, once a month, the prints and posters of works of art they felt illustrated the lectionary passage. This team of adults brought the art to the children of the church school and got them talking about what they noticed in the art and how that art related to the scripture story that day.

Youth Retreats

As a way to build community and communication rapport with our teenagers,
I have found a way to use music and art together. At least once a year we
hold youth retreats or confirmation gatherings where each youth is invited
to bring a favorite song. During the retreat, we make a list of the songs that
have been selected and the name of the person who has brought it. We
randomly select an order of presentation. Before playing the song, crayons
and paper are handed out. Everyone is instructed to draw pictures, write
words, or simply scribble colors according to how music and lyrics move
them. As the song is played, everyone draws. When the song is finished
the person who selected the song is invited to speak about why he or she
brought it to the group. Next, we go around the room and each person
shows his or her picture and explains what has been drawn from the song's
lyrics and music. As people ask questions about the drawings, such as
"Why are those people in bed together? Why did you draw that bottle of
alcohol? What mood does that color express?" various issues are introduced.
Sexuality, alcohol use, alienation, self-esteem, racial tension, violence,
friendships, war, broken relationships, suicide, hopelessness, hopefulness,
and many more themes are present in much of the teens' music. The
discussion offers the adult leaders a chance to raise additional questions or
ask for clarifications about the issues as they appear in the various pictures.
Because we are using their "language" through the music they bring and
the drawings they create, there is much sharing.

Premarital Counseling

Once or twice a year I gather all the couples who will be married in our
church during the coming months for group sessions. Over the course of
three evenings we discuss the issues raised by a premarriage inventory,
practice various communication exercises, and make specific wedding plans.
After our introductions on the first night, we give each couple a large sheet
of paper and some crayons and ask them to draw their definition of a good
marriage. The couples spend about 20 minutes with this, usually drawing
pictures that represent their lives as individuals and as a couple. Their
drawings include self-portraits, pictures of pets, homes, baby carriages,
friendships, activities they do together, and plenty of symbolic hearts, crosses,
and church buildings. We ask each couple to show their picture and tell us
about their drawing. Members of the group will ask questions for clarification.

I keep these pictures and months later show them at the wedding, reminding the couple of how they have defined a good marriage and asking the congregation to support them as they begin their marriage. There is laughter and intense interest when the picture is shown during the ceremony. I have found that incorporating this into the wedding ceremony breaks any tension and nervousness in the sanctuary and helps to call everyone's attention to the meaning of the marriage as developed by the couple. I charge the couple to work at living into their definition of a good marriage.

Adult Education

Another setting in which I use art is an occasional adult education evening. For example, one Lenten evening I divided people into table groups and asked each group to select one of four "I am" passages out of John's Gospel and draw it.

> I am the bread of life.
> I am the light of the world.
> I am the good shepherd.
> I am the vine.

After each group had drawn their picture, they were asked to share it with others, explaining the scripture they worked from and showing how they illustrated the message. This process provided people with an introduction to interpreting a biblical theme through art and encouraged an imaginative interpretation of the theme.

Building Acceptance

By offering members of a congregation experiences with visual arts in several different settings, we were able to build a climate of acceptance for using the visual arts in another important setting of church life: worship. As more and more people in our church gained experience with visual illustration, it became less foreign to them, especially those brought up in the iconoclastic Protestant traditions. After consulting with our worship committee, I slowly began to add visual illustrations to support a few sermons and special worship presentations. On a Sunday after Christmas, for example, I brought in the church's filmstrip projector and showed a filmstrip of the art of Christmas as a way for the congregation to see the Christmas story through the eyes of various religious artists. On another Sunday, I showed four or five slides of the Galilean shore and the old synagogue where Jesus taught to illustrate Luke 4 and the setting where Jesus read from the scroll of Isaiah. During the 150th anniversary year of the church, I showed slides of former church buildings, pastors, and photos of the surrounding area. I illustrated several anniversary-year sermons with these pictures of church members, pastors, and of old theological documents from our archives. One Sunday, at the request of our denomination, church leaders showed a short videotape to kick off a statewide capital funds campaign. The church council agreed to rent a video projector and screen to show the video during worship announcements to stimulate the interest and involvement of our membership. The video program showed the places and ministries our church's gifts would support. People saw and heard the story of this capital campaign rather than simply hearing about it in an oral report.

Whenever visuals were used in worship, I would use every opportunity (such as church committee meetings) to ask our church leaders about what they experienced and what they were hearing from others. They consistently reported that the visuals added to their understanding of what was being presented (sermon, mission moment, announcement) and that the pictures helped hold their interest. By continually asking church leaders about their impressions and inviting them to speak with other members of the congregation to hear their opinions, I was signaling that their input was important and that we would consult with one another along the way.

Video Serving Mission

It was in this context of developing gradual support for using visuals in worship that I worked with our mission committee to visually promote increased awareness of our church's support of various mission projects and to see if that would stimulate greater mission giving from our members. It seemed that if we were going to use new media technologies in worship that we should connect them to the heart of our church's life: our mission in the world. Our mission committee had received a number of videotapes from state, regional, and denominational offices, so we already had material to show people. The mission committee decided to develop a six-week project to determine whether seeing actual videotaped footage of projects supported by our church would increase people's awareness of our wider mission work and therefore their financial support.

They consulted with the diaconate (our worship committee) to be sure they had no problems using video during worship. They thought it was a good idea, since they had been part of every discussion leading to the use of more visuals in worship and evaluating such use. They knew from their conversations with church members that people appreciated the visuals because they helped hold attention while communicating important information. The mission committee then began a process of selecting video clips that could be shown. Since the project promoted the distinctive mission of the United Church of Christ, we decided to use videotapes that had been produced by our denomination to illustrate state, national, and international mission projects. The mission committee decided to show the video during the offering since that was the usual time in our worship when mission concerns were shared. This also established how long the clips could be since the offering usually took no more than three minutes.[3] We looked through the denominational videotapes in our possession for short, one- to three-minute vignettes that told a complete story about a mission project. After narrowing our possibilities to a dozen such clips, the mission committee then selected the six video segments that they felt would best increase our congregation's awareness of its wider mission efforts and would most likely result in an increase in the congregation's financial response. It was decided to show these clips for six weeks after Easter.

Each week during the offering, a committee member or I would position a TV that was hooked up to a videocassette machine in the center aisle of the sanctuary. This central TV was connected to three other TV sets: two in the side aisles and one in the choir loft. During the first service at which we used the video, I used the children's time to explain to the children (and the congregation) why the TV sets were in the sanctuary. I began by asking the children to stand with me near the central TV, on the ground floor of the sanctuary, and asking what they noticed different in the sanctuary that day. They noticed, of course, the TVs. I asked the children if they watched TV, and there was a murmur throughout the congregation that told me the obvious, "Everyone watches TV!" I asked the children about the kinds of programs they watched, and they responded with things like "Disney" and "cartoons" and "movies."

I said that on that day, and during the next few weeks, we would be watching short programs on the TVs, and that these would be different programs from what they might normally watch at home. These were programs that showed people and places that we support with our Sunday offerings. I asked them to pay special attention to these programs because they would be different from what they might usually watch on TV. I said that it might seem strange to have TVs in church, but that they will help us learn something about the people and places our church supports. Next I offered specifics about what they would see, where the scene was from, and explained that our church supported the project with our mission dollars. Later in the service, just before presenting the first video, I explained again to the congregation that our mission committee had selected short programs for us to watch prior to the giving and receiving of the morning offering. For the next six weeks, I said, we would be watching short video segments of projects our church supported with our mission dollars as a way to demonstrate this work to the congregation. The reason I repeated this message several times during the worship service was to prepare people for something new and different.

My experience with churches is that the more people have things explained to them, the better a new thing will be received, especially if there are sound reasons for doing the new thing. For six weeks, I introduced the preoffering video in a similar manner, including a few words about what the congregation would see, so they would have appropriate background for a richer viewing experience. After four weeks of watching the videos on these smaller screens, the only complaint we heard about TVs in the sanctuary was that people in the back could not see the small TV screens. One of our senior church members, a member of the mission committee, then offered to pay for two weeks' rental of a video projector, providing a single projected image on a large 4 ft. x 4 ft. screen. During the course of the mission video project, we solicited feedback from the congregation by a variety of methods, including discussion at various church social events and committee meetings. Questionnaires were distributed to church leaders at committee meetings and included in worship bulletins for several weeks. We asked questions about what people learned from the mission videos, whether they increased their giving as a result of seeing the videos, and whether we should continue to show mission videos. What we learned from their feedback was:

- People were greatly interested in the video segments, thought they remembered the content, were willing to discuss it with others, and gained new insights into the nature of our mission work. One mother reported that she and her children had their first-ever discussion about church missions as a result of their viewing the video clip in church.

- Our members supported continuing the video mission moments on a monthly basis and expressed interest in viewing longer video segments during worship.
- Some were concerned that video not replace either preaching or having missionaries speak to the congregation.
- Some members asked if it were possible to show other church-related ministries in short video segments during worship.
- Many people supported finding a way to get a bigger screen for better viewing of the video.

The committee had hoped that members would increase their mission giving for having seen the mission videos. While most members returned questionnaires saying they did not increase their giving, some did, and our mission giving was up 20 percent during the weeks the videos were shown when compared to the previous six weeks when there were no videos. Our committee credited the video presentation with these positive results. More than that, we learned a lot about the future of multimedia in our church. During the video experiment, we not only learned that the congregation approved of the use of video in worship, but that we had a number of church members who had practical knowledge, interest, and experience with video arts. We also learned that we needed to regularly enlist their talents so that we could have a team of individuals set up and run the equipment, check the sound, and adjust the pictures for the clearest image. Based on my own experience with trying to lead worship and run the equipment, we also learned that we would need a team of individuals comfortable with handling screens, TVs, projectors, and power cords to ensure a smoothly running program.

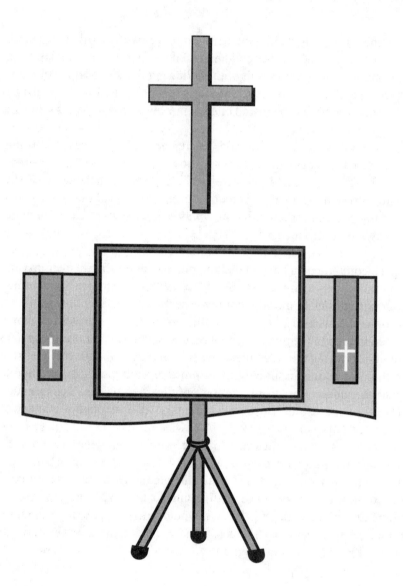

Figure 1

A way to start using imagery in worship is with a portable screen and a projector. Slides, filmstrips, or video may be projected from a short distance in front of the screen. The screen is manually removed after each use.

A third committee, a long-range planning group, joined the diaconate and mission committee in talking about using more media in worship. At the close of our 150th anniversary year, our church council asked a group of people to look ahead five years and begin to set some future goals for our church. This "Towards 2000" visioning committee, because of the success of the video mission project, made it a priority to learn all they could about video technology in worship. Members of this committee visited other churches that were using visuals in worship and reported back at meetings. Some brought back videotapes of these churches to show us what was being done. They invited sales representatives from various audio-video companies to demonstrate different kinds of video projectors and screens. The whole church was notified of these visits so that anyone could come and witness the presentation. The church's interest in this project helped me decide to focus my doctor of ministry program in the use of video and visual arts in worship, and I brought to committee meetings what I learned about through that program.

Since the congregation seemed to be in a mood to experiment, and at the request of the "Towards 2000" visioning group, our diaconate agreed to offer a visually rich worship service for six Saturday evenings. They enlisted a small group of interested persons to work with me to develop six simple multimedia worship services. We selected six worship themes and planned to illustrate those themes with 35 mm slides of religious art, video clips, and a variety of posters and prints. This was yet another step of our gradual, continuing effort to expose people to various visual media in worship. We held our first Saturday evening service in a room in our church's education wing. We hooked a VCR to a TV and showed the music video of Grammy-nominated singer Joan Osborne's 1995 song, "One of Us," where her theme, "what if God was one of us" is illustrated with video of people of all races, shapes, and cultures. The video features a cardboard cutout of Michelangelo's *Creation of Adam* from the Sistine Chapel. There was a hole in the face of God, and various people put their faces into the face of God. After showing the video, I displayed Michelangelo's *Creation of Adam* on an easel so people could compare the music video with a print of the original art. We discussed what we enjoy about being human persons created in God's image and how we experience God's continuing creativity in our lives and in the world in which we live. My introductory comments, the video, and interactive discussion functioned as the sermon for the worship service.

During this six-week experiment with an alternative worship service, I continued to ask all of our church committees for their suggestions, comments, and concerns about bringing more visual multimedia into our worship. At every committee meeting that took place, no matter what the committee's usual responsibilities, I asked people to talk about what we were experiencing. We talked about the technology, people, and resources we would need to start an additional Sunday morning worship service that would feature more extensive use of multimedia in our worship. Over the course of several years of experiments, discussion, and a gradual introduction of visual arts into the whole life of the church, it was clear the membership supported a preparation process for another experimental multimedia worship experience, but this time, during a Sunday morning time slot. As our committees discussed what this new service would be like, they also kept the congregation informed by providing bulletin announcements and newsletter articles about the continuing conversation. They wanted to be sure no one was surprised by anything, and that people understood the conversation was happening. Since we already had two morning services, there was some concern that adding a third service would split the congregation into three worship communities. Yet at the same time, there was a strong interest in developing a completely different sort of worship experience using contemporary music and video as a way to attract a younger group and those who might not be attending any church service.

Further support for a completely different multimedia service came from the "Towards 2000" vision committee, which was coming to understand that adding such a service could help our worship attendance grow from its plateau. They shared with the church how researchers like Lyle Schaller and Bill Easum had shown that multiple worship services, including services that run simultaneously with church school programs and contemporary services that incorporate new music and visuals, all contribute to increasing church attendance and involvement. The committee was building support for trying something new. Their proposal was to create a third Sunday morning worship experience, geared towards youth, young adults, and the parents who normally drop off their children for Sunday school and do not stay for worship. The service would be a completely different experience from the 8:00 and 10:00 services. It would use a simple theme for its message and be built on popular music and video to get the message across. The committee shared what three Sunday morning services would look like through newsletters, bulletin inserts, and discussions with all groups within the church.

8:00 A.M. This service of worship, about 30 minutes in length, is informal with a couple of simple songs, an opening and closing prayer, a unison reading of scripture, and a teaching sermon based on the text.

10:00 A.M. This is the traditional worship with lay readers, children's time, choirs, and organists. The service is conducted in the usual way.

The new third service would be at 9:00 A.M. at the same time as the Sunday school. It would be 30–35 minutes in length and would feature multimedia. A small planning group organizes theme development and technical coordination. A surround sound system is put in place for recorded music. There would be occasional singing with piano and guitar. Scriptures, poems, words to hymns, and sermon points are projected on a screen by means of a computer and a video-data projector. Video clips from popular films, photographs and artworks from CD-ROM resources, and 35 mm slides are used to illustrate the worship theme visually.

After discussion throughout the church, including committees and informal gatherings, the diaconate and church council agreed in the spring to add the media-intensive service the following autumn. They agreed that we would call the service the "U-CC 9" service, which stood for the initials of the church name and the time of the service (Union-Congregational Church, 9:00 A.M.). As the vision for this service caught on, church members began to step forward with donations for needed equipment. One family offered to give the money to purchase a video-data projector, VCR, and a computer for use with the new 9:00 A.M. service. Memorial gifts were used to buy a CD surround-sound system and a rear-projection screen for the projector. More support came when shortly after beginning the new service, another member offered to upgrade our computer equipment to facilitate the new DVD technology.

We had the approval to experiment with a multimedia worship service and the equipment needed to produce it. Now we needed to gather the people resources to begin planning and preparation. We invited people whose "eyes lit up"[4] when we talked at church gatherings about the new "U-CC 9" service. Over the course of the spring and summer, groups of 2 to 12 people met almost weekly to

(continued)

(continued from page 33)

prepare for the first multimedia service that was scheduled for early September. We studied the lectionary together and uncovered worship themes for our first 12 weeks of services. I showed a video clip from a couple of films to show them how we could use short scenes from movies to illustrate our points. People brainstormed songs and video clips that they thought might serve to illustrate the lectionary themes we developed. We worked all summer. Our projector arrived in time for the first worship. Volunteers installed equipment, entered pictures and text into the computer, and ran the equipment during the worship services. We expected 25 persons at our first multimedia service, and 40 came. Attendance doubled, tripled, and now has quadrupled after four seasons. As it continues to grow, our "U-CC 9" media-intensive worship service attendance now regularly equals that of the other two morning services.

Over time, dozens of people became involved in the worship life of their church through this service. These included members and newcomers who:

- wanted to help plan worship themes for the months ahead
- were eager to study scripture and uncover worship themes
- enjoyed listening to music and watching films, and could suggest songs, locate video clips, and find pictures to illustrate the songs that were used
- knew equipment and liked to work with computers, projectors, and sound systems

This transition from using visuals in the church school to adding a media-intensive worship service to our Sunday morning schedule came together in the way that Collins described with his analogy of the flywheel. Efforts to add visuals and multimedia to worship services developed an energy that swept through the congregation as more people throughout the entire church became involved. They grew in their commitment and broadened the ownership of what previously only a few had been doing. Soon it was no longer my project, nor that of just a few people, but something that extended through the entire congregation. We had reached a breakthrough, and there was no turning back.

Leaders Who Learn

A great river has many tributaries. Similarly, there are many sources that contribute to the river of organizational change. As a worship leader working in a congregation, I wanted to be able to define, initiate, guide, and sustain change in that worship. I turned to a number of sources that helped me think about leadership and the process of effective organizational change. What follows is a listing of those tributaries that fed my imagination, stimulated my creative growth, and guided me as I worked with a congregation to develop multimedia-enriched worship. Some of the books written by the authors are included in the bibliography.

Edwin Friedman

Edwin Friedman, a rabbi who brought family systems theory into congregational life, helped me understand what I needed to do as a leader involved with change and transition. Friedman says the leader's work is to be self-defined, playful, and creative. The leader, as the head of the organization, thoughtfully helps move the congregation forward. I found three of his concepts to be particularly helpful:

Self-Differentiated Leadership. Leaders need to be growing, learning, and changing, all the while staying connected with their congregations. Claim the time and resources you need to be the best leader you can. Get out of town and learn something in different environments and come back refreshed and ready. Take a sabbatical, begin a formal learning program, teach a course, or learn a new skill. In the case of multimedia, attend workshops related to the area of media, technology, and learning. Report back to the church often and clearly.

Nonanxious Presence. When change is introduced into a system, disagreements or tensions may arise. The leader needs to stay centered and focused and not take personally the irritations associated with change. Eat right. Exercise. Breathe. Pray, meditate, and cultivate solitude. Relax. Play. Develop your inner core. Monitor how you react to situations and people. Find ways to center and relax even in moments of stress. Find an inner place of calm as you ride the waters of chaos. Trust in the creative power of the Holy Spirit. Breathe again, deeply.

Humor and Paradox. Self-differentiated, nonanxious leaders also maintain a sense of humor. Enjoy jokes. Watch funny movies. Laugh a lot.

Develop a playful imagination. Let your imagination develop many different options. Think "both/and" rather than "either/or." There is always another way, the way of paradox. Learn to develop many options and to make decisions after a wide variety of options are on the table. If a wrong choice is made, learn from it and move on to another one.

Bill Easum

Pastor, consultant, workshop leader, and writer Bill Easum is helping clergy and laity reclaim the lively spirit of the first-century church. I found several of his principles to be particularly useful as I considered ways to help the congregation develop multimedia worship.

Challenges of the 21st-Century. The 20th-century Industrial Age is over and we have already moved into a rapidly changing era defined in part by advances in information technology as well as quantum physics. Yet, Easum says, we organize churches using Industrial-era top-bottom leadership models. As the world around it rapidly changes, the church seems to cling to outdated organizational and leadership models.

Renewed Priorities. Focus pastoral energy on what is essential. Pastors trained in the therapeutic model of pastoral care have filled their time with health-care ministries and committee meetings, and allowed themselves to be manipulated by the controllers of their churches. It is time for clergy to ignite the spirit of their original calling, reset their priorities and dedicate 80 percent of their energy to their most important tasks, and help develop the calling and gifts of the laity for the work of the church.

Indigenous Worship. Learn the language of the people within your congregation and start communicating with it. That means use their music, their movies, and their life-stories as modern parables through which to shine the light of the Gospel.

Making Disciples. Find the people who are spiritually pregnant in a church and be a midwife to them. These are the people within churches who are ready to develop their God-given talents and may be waiting for an invitation or the permission to use their gifts and skills. It is time to make disciples of Jesus Christ and coach and train the people to do the joyful work of the people of God.

Jim Collins

The work of Jim Collins, leader of a management research firm, gave me some tools for understanding how to harness the history of an organization to the horses that pull it into the future. Every church has a lively core of identity that is shaped by the history, traditions, and accomplishments of the past. This core, or life force of the church, wants to move into the future, but it needs somewhere to go. The job of leadership is to stimulate progress while preserving that core identity. Collins's work suggests a way to mine the information that is already embedded in your congregation and to use it for the future.

Core Identity. Identify the core values of your congregation by identifying its history and learning its stories. What are the strengths that have surfaced over time? What are the central purposes of your church that first gave it life, has sustained it over time, and that moves it into the future? What is the central work of this church? What does it do best?

Stimulating Progress. What one area of your organization's life can you stimulate and develop so that it can take off using the energetic source of the core values from which it has grown?

Alignment. Align what you do with your values. As you move forward, be sure that what you are doing fits the core values of the congregation. Be sure the changes you are implementing grow naturally out of your congregation's history and tradition, and out of your church's historic sense of commitment and identity. Your change process then flows naturally from the core identity of the church. When you communicate the changes through the church, the congregation will perceive it as natural change rather than disruptive change.

Margaret Wheatley

Margaret Wheatley, a consultant in organizational behavior, applies what has been learned from the new science of the Quantum Age to leadership and organizations. Three of the concepts she described were particularly helpful to me as I developed strategies for implementing changes in worship methods.

Open-System Thinking. We live in an open universe, not a closed universe. The universe is ever expanding, life systems are forever reorganizing and adapting, and information itself is energy. As I read her applications of open-system thinking to organizations, I thought how we in the church have an open-system theology. Slaves are freed from Egypt and sent to a promised land; Christ is raised from the dead. The impossible became the real. The church is born out of open-system thinking, yet some in the church seem to prefer it live as a closed system of limited resources, limited possibilities, and a downward spiral towards death. It helps to remind one another that our God is a God who opens fresh hope where there was no hope, who frees the captives, and who raises the dead. With God, all things are possible—even with changes in how we worship.

Invisible Fields. Wheatley describes how invisible energy fields, like gravity, exert a field of force that is invisible, yet knowable. Information, she says, is one of those fields. Share as much of it as you can with as many people as possible. The energy of that information will begin to structure and organize itself. How this happens is similar to what Collins talks about: if what you are doing fits the core values and identity of your organization, then the change will follow naturally. Share information about a change with everyone in the organization, continuously and regularly, and this information will begin to structure itself in relationship to that organization in ways that serve the purpose of the organization. Prayer is another one of these energy fields. Prayer is an invisible web of power flowing towards God and to one another. The energy of that information will structure itself into a new thing.

Strange Attractors. Wheatley says there is an attractor built into the very structure of organizations that is continually working to attract new energy and people. It has been there since the beginning. Think of the kinds of people and work your church has done over the years. What is the common theme or component? Why was your church founded? Who were the people attracted to your church then and now? Given this information, how would you define this strange attractor? How does what you are doing or intend to do with multimedia worship relate to this attractor?

Here is an example. The church I serve was the first organized church in the community and sought to reach out to those who were arriving to settle in the territory. From the beginning, the church attracted people from different Protestant backgrounds. The attractor is still in place as the church continues to attract people from different backgrounds, including non-Protestants. The church has always sought to find ways to bring people together rather than to divide them by theological views. How does multimedia worship, or any other change, contribute to the strange attractor already in place in your church?

Paul Tillich, Pierre Teilhard de Chardin, and Pierre Babin
(see bibliography for their works)

Embracing and Resisting Culture. Paul Tillich affirmed that while the church has historically valued high culture of fine art and music, low culture might also be a bearer of God's revelation. He also suggested the Protestant Principle and Catholic Substance idea, later developed by Sally McFague, which describes the challenge of what I call the "both/and" world of both judging and resisting technology, culture, and media, and embracing them. We embrace and resist, criticize and use. We use materials from popular culture and media technologies in worship only after being certain we use them with integrity and humility.

God's Milieu. Pierre Teilhard de Chardin helps us understand the world as a divine milieu in which God has created spirit and matter together. God's life is experienced in the matter of existence, in the culture in which we live, and in the world around us. We participate in God as we acknowledge the Holy Presence in our midst. Teilhard's writing contributes to the ways that we uncover messages about God in the creative material of our world.

Print and Electronic Culture. Pierre Babin's definition of the difference between print culture and electronic culture and what that means for the church and its teaching ministry, worship life, and evangelism, has helped me develop a rationale for using multimedia technologies in worship. He helps us understand the transition our society has been making for over 40 years from print culture to electronic culture, and how the church needs to keep pace with these changes in order to more effectively evangelize.

Eileen Crowley-Horak

During the course of this writing, Crowley-Horak sent me her completed doctoral dissertation for the faculty at Union Theological Seminary in New York. Crowley-Horak studied our congregation for her work about media art as a new liturgical art form. During her visits with our congregation, she helped us understand that our media production teams are creative artists who are engaging God's word in fresh new ways. Crowley-Horak brought to our attention that we were accomplishing some of the work that media theorists thought was possible. She provided our team with new vocabulary for understanding they are "ritual symbolic engineers" and "cultural poachers" who are inventing a new form of worship that has integrity, aesthetic quality, prophetic edge, and accountability.

Developing Personal Models

In addition to working with the resources listed above, I found it helpful to develop my own theological foundation to support my thinking and to find a living, natural metaphor that could be another source for imaginative thought.

Develop a scriptural and theological foundation as you build your thinking. For me, three main scriptural ideas and one theological concept formed the four corners of this foundation as I worked to develop multimedia worship with a congregation.

Word and Light. Genesis tells us that at the beginning of creation, God paired word and light. Hovering over the swirling chaos, God said (with words), "Let there be light." Later on in the New Testament, John recalls the "word" was present at the beginning, how through it "light" came into the world, and then that "Word became flesh." Through word and light comes the mystery of the incarnation of God's love. This word, light, and flesh become a kind of holy trinity that act upon one another when we worship. Our words, the pictures we project by means of light on a screen, and our bodies, all interact in multimedia worship.

The Body of Christ. The apostle Paul told the church that we are individually part of one body, and to "each is given the manifestation of the Spirit for the common good" (1 Cor. 12:7). Fashioned as it is in the body of Christ, the church is called to identify, celebrate, and call forth the individual gifts of the people into the mission of the Bible. Producing multimedia worship is an opportunity to invite into the life of the church a wide array of artistic gifts.

A People in Transition. The early Hebrews were a people who experienced God's breaking into history to free them from their slavery and oppression and to set them on a journey towards a new land flowing with milk and honey. These Hebrews were a people in transition, moving from one place to another. They had to leave Egypt and travel by an unknown route towards their destination. Many were fearful, others grumbled, still others doubted. Yet by wise leadership and the Holy Presence, the people were able to fulfill their mission and arrive at the promised land. Along the way, these transitional Hebrews became a people. Through the Ten Commandments they became a people of the covenant and gained a new name, "Israel." As we in the church move along our journey, our route may not be clear, yet in all things we learn to trust God's leading.

Theology and Theophany. As I have wandered through this land of media, worship, and the church, I have learned how a print orientation has left us with many words about God or theology. We have reduced *theology* to mean lots of words about God. Worship is full of words in bulletins, sermons, hymns, and prayers. We are well trained in the use of oral and print communication. Many of today's seminary-based critics of technology in worship come out of the wordy print culture of reading, writing, speaking, and listening, and out of iconoclastic Protestantism that promotes words over images as a primary worship language. But what about the language of light known to us in picture and in other things we see? What about biblical concepts like *epiphany*, (meaning "manifestation") or *theophany* (meaning "God light" or "to show God")? In the Bible, theophanies were at those times when God's voice and bright light brought a clear message to the people. I think of the theophany experiences of Moses at the burning bush, Jesus at the transfiguration, and Paul on the road to Damascus. Screens and projectors that display pictures, words, and movie clips can serve God's light, just as preached sermons and printed prayer books can serve God's word.

A natural metaphor grew out of this theological foundation. It helped me think about what I was doing from a completely different perspective, and it helped me explain in simple terms how change is a natural process. The questions I ask are questions I asked of myself and which you may ask of yourself as you lead a transition in your church. For me, the garden provided a metaphor of change. The church is like a garden (see the vineyard metaphor in Isa. 5). What are the fruits you seek? What are the sweet fruits God wants? What, then, are you going to be planting? Where are you going to be planting? What needs to be cleared away to prepare the soil? What needs to be added to the soil? What fertilizer do you need? What else will the seeds need? What skills and gifts will you need at different stages of growth? When do you expect the harvest, who will help, and who will join in the celebration feast?

Building Momentum

Our church's process of change took several years to develop. As I look back on it, I can isolate a number of the incremental pushes that built our momentum and moved our flywheel until it has gained energy of its own. I present them as recommendations and questions for you to think about as you consider a process of change within your own congregation.

- Examine your own commitment to the community you serve. Are you willing to enter a process of introducing the visual arts into your church's life and guide people in a learning process about it? Do you truly believe the time is right for your church either to integrate multimedia into existing worship services or to start an additional service that uses multimedia resources?

- Identify your congregation. What age groups are represented within your congregation? Approximately how many people are in what age groupings? How many will be in those age categories in five years? In 10 years? How might the age of your congregation impact decisions you make now about worship change?

- Which persons in your congregation have interests, skills, and talents in multimedia and technology?

- How is your neighborhood or region changing? What are other churches doing to respond to similar changes? What worship changes do you notice them making? What styles of worship speak the language of the people within your area?

- Start a conversation about the history, strong traditions, and historic foundation of your congregation. Gather older members and talk about the ways the church navigated through the technological changes of the 19th and 20th centuries. What were some of those changes? What transitions did the church make during those years? Why did they make that transition? What happened to churches that did not? Were any of those transitions similar to transitions that are being made now? Try to discover examples of your church's resiliency during those transitional times. Does the church still demonstrate that resilience? What about your congregation's history and tradition will help it move through coming transitions?

- Talk with other church leaders about the core values of your congregation. What would you say are the three or four values the church has historically held at all costs? Come up with a list of words or phrases that describe your church. Ask people at a committee meeting to come up with a similar list. What words or phrases commonly surface from the group's lists? What do these words tell you about the core values of your congregation? Think about the changes the church has made over the years that have had significant impact upon the life and health of the congregation. How did these changes grow out of the core value system of the congregation?

- Talk together about what attracts people to your church. What attracted them long ago, and what attracts them now? Is there any difference over the years? Is there a pattern that you can see? What does this say about the core of your congregation?
- Claim a vision for the future. Where do you want your church to be in 5, 10, or 25 years? Engage the church leadership body in a similar process of seeing into the future and identifying a vision. Meet regularly with a core group of interested people. Continue to talk together about what you are learning. Talk together, dream together, and clarify your goals and visions.
- Identify the one single area of your church's life that has the greatest impact upon the life of the church. How much time do your leaders devote to making that part of your church's life the best it can be? What nonessential activities could be stopped in order to devote more energy to that single area of greatest important to the life of your church?[5] What changes might be needed to improve upon the quality of that single area of your church's life?
- Identify a small number of lay leaders in your church who you think share your interest and excitement. Who are the core leaders within your church who are ready to move forward with you? Who are the leaders who would best respond to incorporating visuals in worship?
- Get yourself informed: read the authors who are writing about change in the church, especially the books and periodicals addressing worship, technology, and church growth. Seek out the writers who are teaching about leadership and organizations and how to navigate through times of rapid change. Buy multiple copies of the books and periodicals you and others are reading and share them for reading and later discussion.
- Go to workshops that discuss the issues you are excited about. Visit churches already using multimedia in worship and report back. Take pictures or videotape of what other churches are doing. Interview friends and family who may be attending those churches to learn what you can from them. Ask them what multimedia their churches use, how they decided to use them, how they are used, and how it was financed. Ask about problems and surprises they encountered. Find out what effect the new technology has had upon attendance, worship style, and visitors.
- Learn about electronic media and equipment. Find out what other churches are doing. Learn about the positive and negative experiences

they have had. Think about what you might do that might be similar to what they are doing and what will be different. What kind of projectors are they using? Are they using computers? How have they integrated media hardware and screens into their sanctuary? What has happened as a result?

- Do a technology survey of your church. List all the ways that your church has utilized technological innovations. Examples include telephone, microphones, central air and heat, indoor plumbing, grape juice in communion, printing equipment, clocks, movie and filmstrip projectors. What are some technologies the church has not chosen to use? Why is that? When should the church resist technological innovation, and why? When should the church embrace it, and why?
- Investigate the electronic multimedia technology already available to you at your church, such as projectors, screens, and computers. Brainstorm what more you might need. Check into prices. Study what is out there. Bring it before the congregation as part of a shopping list of future needs for the church, and explain why certain things are needed.
- Assemble the visual artists and photographers in your church and talk about ways to incorporate visuals into the learning settings of the church.
- Begin a Bible study by bringing one of the large pictures that has been hanging somewhere in the church or that you found in one of the closets. Ask the group what they see. Have them do three things: identify the main characters in the picture and decide what is happening in the picture. Next, notice any significant details that point to the meaning of the picture. Finally, talk about how they interpret the meaning of the picture and how they might relate it to the Bible study. How did looking at the picture open their imaginations?
- Begin introducing visuals into worship. Show a small number of 35 mm slides or images from filmstrips. Start simply and appropriately. At Christmas, show slides of Christmas art or of a painting or sculpture that illustrates a point in a sermon.
- Utilize video resources. Bring in a TV and a VCR. Show a minute of footage from a recent youth retreat. Show a minute of a recent church luncheon or dinner. Show the church school kids working on an art project. Use the offering time wisely: instead of an offertory, show a video mission moment.
- Keep assembling the people who are interested in various aspects of what you have done together and keep them talking and thinking. These

action people will keep pushing for change through the church. Speak before the various groups in your church to communicate the dreams, the visions, and the hopes that you and your committees have been developing over time. Keep the vision alive in monthly committee meetings. Keep all groups within the congregation informed of the vision and the dream.

- Train youth and adults to put images to music. Discuss the music they listen to and practice uncovering important themes. At a youth meeting, ask group members to tear out magazine pictures that illustrate a particular song and tape them to pieces of paper. Play the song and ask members to show the images. Have some fun talking about why certain pictures were selected to go with certain words. Get out 35 mm slide collections and have them build a slide show around a song. Go on the Internet and have them find pictures they think illustrate the messages of the song. You are beginning to develop media artists within your congregation.

- Start a film group to view movies and discuss the themes found in contemporary film. Begin to train one another to see how certain scenes might illustrate certain biblical stories or theological themes. Discover how cultural material reflects or contrasts with gospel messages. Illustrate sermons with verbal references to film, TV, and music. Describe a scene and bring it to life. Mention that sometime soon you would like to be able to show the scene during a sermon so the congregation could experience it for themselves. Follow through and arrange to show a video clip or a snippet of a song during a sermon. Give the congregation little tastes of multimedia in worship.

- Think about the architecture of your worship space. What does it teach about God and how does it organize a style of worship? What is it saying about how your congregation approaches God in worship? What changes might you make to the architecture to incorporate projecting words and pictures before the congregation? Is there a way to temporarily reduce the light coming into the sanctuary by installing shades or draperies? Is there a projector light bright enough that it can overpower any ambient light? Will you have to use a projector at an evening service instead of during daylight hours? Where might you place a screen with the least interruption to architectural features of your sanctuary? Is it possible to use a screen on a temporary basis? Where might be the place for a permanent screen?

- Encourage a teaching approach to worship. Build a community of teachers and learners. Provide outlines of weekly sermons in the worship bulletin. Add drawings, photographs, or quotations to illustrate the sermon. Begin to build a learning community by focusing attention on a variety of visual resources during a sermon.
- If you are not already doing so, think about what would happen were you to hold worship at the same time as Sunday school so that young-adult parents can worship while their children are in class.
- Organize church leadership to use time more efficiently. To have the time and energy to begin a new program means worship leaders may have to give something else up. Consider developing a style of group-based ministry, where small groups within the church are trained to provide various ministries such as hospital and home visits, premarriage counseling, and similar work. Wonder about what the pastor does that other lay leadership could be doing as expressions of their Christian calling. Develop group ministries and train people to do the work of the church, freeing the pastor to do the worship work and keep a creative edge. Consider how laity can provide such ministries as premarital sessions, nursing home and home visitations, home communions, new member meetings, confirmation sessions, hospital visits, and so forth.
- Pause. After a period of using visuals, take a step back to evaluate. Ask church groups what they think about the ways the church has been moving lately. How are people responding to the conversation and experiments with visuals? Take a few weeks off, pausing any forward progress. Do not talk about or use any multimedia in church. Do things as you usually did, without visuals, and wait to hear from others. You may discover the momentum is already in place and many are still energized by the vision and want to develop next steps.

As I look back over these many steps that we took as we added visuals to worship, and added a successful multimedia-intensive service to our Sunday morning schedule, I realize that the whole church has invested a lot of time and energy into the project. It has brought fresh new energy into the life of a church that, at 157 years old, would more predictably be declining and doing the same old things. Often those who hear about our multimedia worship will ask us how many hours a week it takes to develop. Sometimes I think their question comes out of their fear that there will not be enough time, people, or resources to transform worship into a "vigorous" and "vivid" experience, as the Rev. Jump dreamed of so long ago. I have found the opposite to be true. Adding multimedia worship to our church has stimulated a living spring of energy. I have found that multimedia worship has brought us a rich wellspring of creative people, generous financial support, and a whole lot of new life to our church. After almost 30 years of ordained ministry, I am able to share my passion for music, art, and film with others who are equally as excited about using them to communicate to and for God in worship.

Whether you are transitioning into using more visuals to illustrate or support your worship, or are intent upon developing a stand-alone media-intensive worship experience with a full use of film, music, and art, one big question is how and where to find the media. In the next chapter we will think together about how to use contemporary music, film, and other visual arts to illustrate, support, and interact with your worship message and experience.

Chapter 3

Learning to Use Film, Art, and Music

A clergy colleague tells the story of a Midwestern church whose worship services at the turn of the last century were conducted in the congregation's native Norwegian tongue. When some members requested that services be conducted in their new language, English, and the leaders refused, they left to form an English-speaking congregation. That congregation continues to the present day. What happened to the Norwegian-speaking congregation? "No one knows," says my friend.[1] This story is typical of the experience of many congregations in this country that in the late 19th century began to replace their native worship language with the new 20th century worship language. Churches either provided services in both languages or closed their doors.

We are now in the midst of another language transition, although usually we do not think of it as such. Our native worship language is expressed in printed words and oral communication, while the new language of the 21st century, which has not quite made it into our worship, is expressed with visual imagery and popular music punctuated with short bursts of spoken information. The new language, with which most of us are familiar, comes into our homes through many media. According to the Kaiser Family Foundation, the typical American family has two TVs, three audio tape players, three radios, two VCRs, two CD players, one video game player, and one computer. Children and teens listen to music between three and four hours a day and are in front of electronic screens (TVs, computers, and video games) four and a half hours a day.[2] U.S. culture was well into the transition from print culture to electronic culture in the 1960s and '70s, as people devoted increasing amounts of time to watching TV and listening to the radio and decreasing amounts of time to reading books, magazines, and newspapers. Since that time, the number of hours devoted to electronic media continues to rise, with TV viewing increasing by a third more hours, time spent listening to music nearly quadrupling, and reading continuing to decline.[3] With the development of home video, personal computers, the Internet, and video games, people are devoting even more hours seeing, hearing, and expressing their electronic language.

Nearly a decade ago, Doug Adams, professor of Christianity and the arts at Pacific School of Religion, understood the challenges this growing divide between word-centered worship and a people who speak a new language would bring: "If our worship, preaching and teaching remain largely verbal, they may as well be spoken in Latin for they will not be remembered by the majority of the population whose language is now the visual arts. If we communicate with the visual arts, then the Word will be remembered."[4]

Learning a New Language

Tex Sample, retired professor of church and society at Saint Paul School of Theology, has committed much of his recent teaching and writing to helping the church understand that it must begin to learn the language of today's electronic culture in order to communicate with people more effectively. He has noted how "electronic culture and the screen introduce an entire range of practices" including what he calls an experience of "visualization" which "takes on even greater force when combined with percussive images and sound as beat."[5] Both he and Adams have taught the importance of bringing into worship the language of our time. By bringing into worship the films that people watch and the music they listen to, worship leaders (1) capture attention by the sheer surprise of bringing the world out there into the domain of the church, (2) shine the light of God through that media to help it tell a story about God's creative and transformative Word, and (3) send people back into their world freshly alert to ways that the Word of God works in and through the world in which they live, including the music they hear and the movies they watch, calling them to mission and ministry.

Yet another reflection on the powerful opportunities the new language presents is written by Frank Burch Brown, professor of religion and the arts at Christian Theological Seminary, who thinks that "marrying gospel insights and liturgical actions to a musical or linguistic medium that was originally secular in sound and purpose is an art in itself."[6] This is exactly what "liturgical media artists"[7] do when they take pieces of movies and music and fit them into the sacred stories of God's saving love active in a broken world. By using the language of electronic multimedia, worship leaders can capture attention, tell God's story, and send people back out into the world more alert to God's action in that world. Here are some examples of how this can happen through the use of film or music.

One of the first films we used in worship was a scene from *Austin Powers: International Man of Mystery* (1997), a spoof of the 1960s James Bond movies. Using a short scene from a film so popular with the American audience and probably seen by many in the congregation immediately captures attention. Many will wonder, "How can they find something of spiritual value in a film like this?" The light-hearted humor of the scene, the familiarity of most young adults with the Austin Powers character, and a curiosity about what this has to do with church opens a communication opportunity more powerful than most oral illustrations. Towards the end of this James Bond-spoof, 1960s British spy figure Austin Powers confronts a character known as Dr. Evil, who suggests that Powers's 1960s-era spirit of freedom has failed. Powers disagrees by saying that freedom has not failed and that "right now we have freedom *and* responsibility. It's a very groovy time."

The way that we used this short clip in worship was to introduce a series of sermons on the Ten Commandments. Our media team showed the clip, and then I explained how the Ten Commandments is a covenant between God and people that is freely entered into by both parties, and requiring the fulfillment of certain ethical responsibilities. In a way, Austin Powers explained the nature of the Ten Commandments by introducing the concept of freedom and responsibility. God gives us both freedom and a responsibility to live together by the specific ethical standards expressed by the Ten Commandments. Applying a scene from a goofy movie like *Austin Powers* to a central topic of the life of faith immediately captures attention and prepares a congregation for a clear message. The electronic language of a motion picture supplements verbal illustrations to convey an important point about our life together. It offers a bilingual experience combining the native speaking-reading worship language with the new electronic language found in movies.

Another way that electronic language effectively communicates to today's congregations is in its ability to powerfully show, through the use of amplified sound and large image, some aspect of our sacred stories. One year our church's media team developed a 17-week series about the twelve disciples and the women who followed Jesus. To begin the series, we set the historical context for Jesus' calling the disciples in Galilee by explaining about the Roman occupation of Palestine. Jesus was calling his disciples to follow him in the midst of a very cruel military situation. While we might think the calling of Jesus' followers was at a beautiful, peaceful Galilean shore, it was in fact accomplished against the backdrop of warfare and destruction. The people who followed Jesus did so in a time of rebellion, resistance to Roman rule, and under the threat of death.

To set a realistic backdrop for the time and historical setting, we showed a scene found near the opening of the film *Gladiator* (2000). Unlike the *Austin Powers* scene that featured dialogue between two characters in the film, there is only action in this scene. In just a couple of minutes of a film sequence, we saw the fearsome power of the Roman legions as they organized themselves in a great valley, lined up with their weapons and shields, and waited to move forward. Catapults slung huge fireballs into the forest where Goths gathered to defend their homeland. As the fireballs exploded in the forest, the Goths were forced to charge from their hiding places. Roman archers then shot wave after wave of arrows at them, until they came crashing into the front lines to grapple with shielded, helmeted, ax-wielding soldiers. We stopped the scene right there, before anyone actually saw any of the ensuing mayhem. I stood next to the screen, which was showing the still image of the final frame of our movie scene, with the Romans and Goths converging upon each other. I told the quiet congregation that the Roman army was in fact what they had just seen: a well-trained, devastatingly powerful force able to subdue any and all opponents. These same forces occupied Galilee and Jerusalem during the years when Jesus and his followers preached, healed, and taught. The film clip not only captured everyone's attention, but it dramatically illustrated the New Testament context for Jesus' life and ministry, and how he, and others, would die at those Roman hands in a few short years. A preacher could tell this story, probably better than I can write it, but to tell it combining the electronic language of the modern motion picture with a verbal description, we increase the emotional impact upon a learning congregation.

A third way that electronic language contributes to our worship is in the way it can stimulate continuing connections between the worshipers and the world in which they live. As mentioned earlier, we have used nearly 250 songs by popular artists in our multimedia worship service. We have used the works of singers like Willie Nelson, Gloria Estefan, Celine Dion,

Joan Baez, REM, U2, Bill Withers, Alabama, Jewel, Sheryl Crow, Boyz II Men, Metallica, Garth Brooks, John Mellencamp, Michael W. Smith, Billy Joel, Shania Twain, Ben Harper, Tom Petty, Amy Grant, Creed, Dave Matthews, and dozens of other singers and songwriters. We have used their songs to illustrate worship themes by lectionary, topic, and season.

Members volunteer to find pictures that illustrate both the meaning of the song's lyrics, and how they understand what the song means in relationship to the worship theme, or how the worship theme relates to the lyrics of the song. The pictures our team selects to accompany the songs include original photography, photographs from the Internet, scanned images from 35 mm slides, filmstrips, and photographs, art from purchased resources, and original artwork (drawings from Sunday school children that were scanned into the computer).

During an annual stewardship campaign, someone thought that the song "Kind and Generous" by Natalie Merchant offered a good message about giving. The song is about the singer's gratitude for the many gifts someone has shared with her. Such gratitude was understood to be similar to our gratitude to God for many blessings showered upon us. The repetitive refrain, "I want to thank you, thank you, thank you, thank you . . ." offered a number of creative interpretive possibilities. One of our younger teenagers asked children in the church school to draw pictures of things for which they were thankful. The children colored pictures of their pets, families, homes, food, and church. The teen that was producing this song for our worship scanned the pictures into his computer. Several children drew pictures of the earth itself as something for which they were thankful, and with the help of computer software, these particular images were animated to appear to spin on the screen. Some of the song lyrics were posted on the pictures so the viewers were sure to understand the song. This program of still and moving imagery was put together with Microsoft's PowerPoint software as a slide show, copied to a CD-RW computer disk, and brought to church. The congregation's attention was captured by the cute yet poignant images drawn by their children, and the music drove home the message that we can both be grateful for generosity and generous in response to gratitude. More than that, members reported that when they heard the song on the radio during the following weeks, they thought about how the song had been tweaked at church to bring a message of gratitude to God and of giving in return. When they heard the song, they now heard something about God.

Practicing the Language

Using multimedia in worship and communicating with electronic language involves artistic combinations of music and visuals. There are endless possibilities for combining words, pictures, videos, live music, and recorded music to accent, illustrate, support, and interact with sermons and other acts of worship. Before working to produce media and incorporating it into worship, leaders do well to think about the extent to which they will use multimedia in their various worship settings.

Illustrating with Media

A common function for worship multimedia is to use it to illustrate some part of a worship service. This usually involves a minimal use of media, perhaps using the screen and projecting equipment on an occasional basis, maybe once a month, until a congregation becomes more comfortable with regular use. When used, illustrative media might be projected on a screen once or twice in the course of a worship service. Examples of occasional, illustrative media are:

- showing pictures of a youth-group retreat during the preservice announcements
- displaying a short video of a mission project your church supports as a way to introduce the offering
- using a short video clip from a popular movie to begin a sermon
- showing a picture of a map to help illustrate a Bible lesson
- displaying lyrics to hymns and songs, words to prayers and scripture passages, or a sermon outline

A way to illustrate some part of worship in a manner acceptable to most everyone in a congregation is to develop a short program recognizing a confirmation group or the recent high-school graduates. A recent confirmation class selected the Green Day song, "The Time of Your Life" to be the soundtrack for a display of their photographs. We asked them to bring a baby picture and a current picture, which were scanned into the computer and entered into a PowerPoint slide program. We also included photographs of one of their mission trips, along with pictures from a class session, taken with the church's digital camera. The program opened and closed with the words to 1 Corinthians 12:27, "Now you are the body of Christ and individually members of it." During the course of the two and one-half minute song, we showed some 30 pictures at six-second intervals. Three generations of family members who attended the service took delight in the presentation, which served as a multimedia introduction to the members of the group about to be confirmed.

Illustrative media light up or illuminate some aspect of a worship experience. They serve to make something clear. Illustrative media may be used at any point during a worship service, including during a sermon, to help the congregation see what is being described. Traditional and blended worship services can easily accommodate this use of media because the use of the media does not alter the fundamental character of worship. Illustrative media contribute to oral-print culture worship, and serve a text-based, spoken and written communication style.

Multimedia Intensive Worship

Where illustrative media may be incorporated into most any kind of worship experience, a more intensive use of media might require a separate worship service because it uses more electronic language than oral and print language. What is fundamentally different about this use of media is that the media, which have been carefully selected for their artistic relevance to the worship theme and message, shape the message. The silver screen and sacred story become a multidimensional art form. Imagery is allowed to represent itself, rather than being a servant of words. While there is an interaction between words and visuals, such worship becomes "trilingual" in the sense that it uses oral presentation, print communication, and the electronic language of audiovisual media. This intensive use of multimedia in worship allows for experiments with electronic language through the use of music of all types and styles, film clips from a wide number of movies, and special animation effects on the screen. I recommend that those wishing to experiment with this form of worship do so by adding this trilingual service to the worship schedule rather than attempting to blend it into an existing service. This service will appeal to those most comfortable using electronic language. Those who are not visual learners or who appreciate oral-print oriented worship will generally not respond well to this style of service. Those who will respond favorably, however, are the visual learners and those who are looking for God in the midst of the world in which they live and the electronic language that they speak. It is, as Crowley-Horak states in her study of worship use of such media, "a hybrid art form, a new creation that is the offspring of the art-and-technology marriage of the 20th century."[8]

An example of a multimedia-intensive service is one that grew out of our 17-week series on Jesus and the women and men who followed him. Our worship theme was simply "Matthew the Tax Collector," and the scripture we organized the service around was Matthew 9:9, "As Jesus was walking along, he saw a man called Matthew sitting at the tax booth; and he said to him, 'Follow me.' And he got up and followed him." We used a variety of media to create the worship experience: a scene from a Bible movie, three different songs representing three different styles of popular music that were set to visual imagery, and a piece of baroque art. A central piece of media art our team prepared paired the brilliant composition of Caravaggio's baroque canvas, *The Calling of St. Matthew* (a digital image obtained from a purchased art CD) with the Beatles' sarcastic song of a tax collector, "Taxman." We designed this to help the congregation understand both Matthew's unpopularity as a tax collector, and what he had to give up to follow Jesus. Prior to the opening of the worship service, several CD musical selections, chosen for the way they related to the theme of being loved, accepted, and called to a new reality, were played over the sound system while a "loop" of announcements, 21 slides which cycled every 10 seconds for 10 minutes, were shown on the screen. These announcements included reminders of events at church during the coming week as well as thoughtful quotations taken from stewardship resources, since we were in the midst of the fall stewardship campaign. The service opened at 9 A.M. with a verbal welcome, and then the words to a call to worship and an invocation were shown on the screen for all to see and read aloud. At the Amen, people sat down and we played, without introduction, the song "Excuse Me, Mr." by Ben Harper. Members of the youth group found 25 pictures to show as the song was played. They selected images that depicted various themes in the song, such as polluted air and water, homelessness, and hungry children. Since the song raised questions about how we would respond to these social problems, we thought it could fit our stewardship theme of the week before, while also serving as a transition into our new theme. We linked the story of Matthew with stewardship by showing the Caravaggio painting during a key line from the song: "It's the mister like you . . ." Looking at the painting at that moment, the viewer could understand that Matthew, seated at the tax collector's table, put "us to shame" by his lowly profession. As the song ended, we projected the words from 2 Corinthians 8:7, "We want you to excel also in this generous undertaking." The final slide was a lead-in to the first part of my message, the purpose of which was to connect our stewardship with Jesus calling forth our gifts.

Next, I introduced two short video clips from the film *Jesus* (2000) that showed Matthew in his tax collector's office, and later showed Peter's disgust with Matthew and his profession. After the short scenes were shown, I commented about the way people treated tax collectors with contempt for their collaboration with the Roman occupation, yet Jesus called one of them to follow him. This introduced the next song, "Taxman," by the Beatles, during which we used Caravaggio's painting as the single visual image to accompany the song as it played, as mentioned above. By using the editing capability of the computer software program, we highlighted specific parts of the painting. We showed Peter and Jesus standing at the door, next a close-up of Matthew's face as he looked at them, and then faces of some of the other characters in the painting. As the music played, we matched 21 different views of the painting to the song's lyrics, allowing both the painting and the song to illustrate the scriptural account of the calling of Matthew. When the song was finished, we kept showing the full painting on the screen, and I pointed out some of the details the artist presented as his interpretation of the scripture. I concluded by focusing on the choice Matthew was asked to make, to choose between God and his job, between the kingdom of the world and the kingdom of God, between self-fulfillment or fulfilling God's kingdom.

We showed another video scene from the *Jesus* movie, of Jesus teaching about the difference between the treasures of the earth and the treasures of heaven (Matt. 6:19-21), and then we showed one more painting, *St. Matthew and the Angel* by Guido Reni. As it was displayed on the screen, I spoke of how Matthew's conversion from tax collector to disciple might seem a radical step, yet he simply traded masters. He turned his taxman skills of accounting for money into a way to account for the earthly work of Jesus by recording that work in the Gospel of Matthew. I offered a one-minute review of the sorts of themes Matthew recorded in his Gospel, including the story of Jesus' birth and the arrival of the magi with their gifts. At that I turned the question to the congregation, and asked how they match their God-given talents and gifts with God's calling them to be a follower. We then played the song "Change Your Mind" by a group called

Sister Hazel. A laywoman in the church found 29 visual images to illustrate the words to this song, including the line, "if you want to be somebody, change your mind." She was able to communicate the biblical concept of repentance, of turning around or changing one's mind, through her choice of imagery used to accompany the song. We are called to turn from our former ways and follow Jesus, sharing our gifts with others, like Matthew did so long ago. When the song ended, we moved into a time of prayer and the Lord's Prayer. The entire worship service lasted around 35 minutes and involved a series of interactions between worship theme, the creative material contained in a painting, a movie, two songs, and photography illustrating one of the songs, a team of church members, a preacher, and a worshiping congregation.

You may find worshipers will grow to welcome selected multimedia in traditional worship. They may not welcome, however, a more media-intensive worship service, such as the one described above, with a larger use of multimedia. Worship leaders may need to consider adding a separate, multimedia-intensive worship service to their worship schedule.

Gaining Fluency

As with learning to communicate with any new language, worship leaders will want to develop their electronic language skills as they begin to think and speak it as another worship language. Most all of us are familiar with the electronic language of film, TV, and music. Some are already fluent in the language and know exactly how to interact with such media in presenting a worship message. Others, like myself, who have been trained in using oral language to create pictures with words, have a more difficult time thinking visually. We have learned to think in words rather than to think of pictures that could communicate our concept. We expect words alone to pull the burden of communication, and have not thought much about harnessing pictures with words to share the load. On the other hand, those already fluent with electronic language and who easily think in terms of musical and cinematic illustration may sometimes miss the deeper theological content and meaning in the media they experience. Learning to see a work of art or a film, or to listen to a piece of music are necessary skills to develop if we who speak the different languages of word, picture, film, and theology are to work with others in creating multimedia art that serves our worship purposes.

I frequently hear clergy and laity say that they know nothing about art. One of the legacies of an emphasis upon literacy is that many of us have lost the art of seeing a work of art. We have so emphasized words that we have lost the ability to hear what images are saying to us. Hundreds of years ago, worshipers knew exactly how to read a work of art by paying attention to the well-known symbols associated with religious figures. They knew the subject of the painting was Peter because he was holding a ring of keys. They understood Paul often held a sword and a book. Mary was the woman with an open book and an angel kneeling in front of her. Learning to read art so we can quote it in worship requires we open ourselves to it. As art educator Sister Wendy Beckett writes, "Looking at art is one way of listening to God."[9] How shall we learn to see?

Theologian John Dillenberger writes, "A discipline of seeing does not come by being told how to see, though that may be helpful, even necessary; it comes primarily by seeing and seeing and seeing over and over again."[10] Part of his program for reintroducing the arts into the churches is to have clergy and laity find opportunities to interact with the visual arts. It was through the guidance of my wife, a lover of the arts, that I was first introduced to some of the great art museums of the world. She introduced me to wonderful art, and with her help, I began to notice things about art that grew my faith. I began to see how religious art, in particular, because of its obvious connection to scriptural passages and themes, could enhance worship experiences. As a result, I have gained an appreciation and familiarity for art in ways that helps me use it in the worship setting. You might remember hearing about a popular poster that said, "Expose yourself to art." That is what you need to do to train yourself and a worship team in the use of visual arts. There are many ways to do this. When traveling, try to visit art museums. Learn all you can about the art in the museum by renting the museum's audio guide to hear how the experts interpret various works. Or, you might hire a personal guide, or tag along with a group. Museums usually provide free literature that helps explain the history and background of some of their featured pieces. Use this material or other written guides to the art you will see (often available at public libraries).

Interactive museums such as Disney's Epcot Center at Orlando, Chicago's Museum of Science and Industry, or Cleveland's Rock and Roll Hall of Fame and Museum help us learn to see while experiencing a range of other multimedia-learning techniques. Visits to museums help us learn to see in new ways, as well as experience educational multimedia uses of art, photography, music, and video. One need not travel far from home to gain experience with the arts. Watching films and plays with church members and friends helps us learn to see and experience art in new ways. By inviting teachers, artists, photographers and musicians to speak at church about the arts, the whole congregation can learn how to incorporate music, film, drama, art, sculpture, and photography into the life of the church.

A lot can be learned in the comfort of one's home too. Watch public TV programs on the arts. Tune to music channels and see how music videos are produced. Notice the edits, the use of color, the linking of lyric to image, and how sometimes lyric and images do not seem to fit. Observe newscasts, and notice how TV producers use various visuals and music to grab your attention or to anchor a theme. Study the commercials. Notice how they link music with picture. Notice how quickly pictures change from one image to the next, and notice what is moving on your screen. Think about what makes the visual experience pleasing, or persuasive, and notice what it is that you do not like about the use of imagery. Notice how old songs are used in creative new ways. Turn off the sound to watch the pictures alone, or turn on the sound and listen to it without looking at the pictures. Recognize how sound and image, when combined, change each other, and serve to communicate a message. How do the images and sounds combine to bring a persuasive impact?

Rent movies or borrow them from a public library. Watch for religious content and theological themes. Learn how to talk about what you watch with others. Experiencing multimedia through TV, radio, and film, and talking about it with others, helps create a community of learners who are excited about the world in which they live, and who are seeking to develop and understand their religious faith in relationship with this world.

A way of interpreting any work of visual art, including photographs, films, paintings, and architecture, is to follow a "form-content-meaning" process.[11] Essentially the viewer identifies three things:

- The form of what you are looking at. Simply identify the kind of art it is (for example, painting, photography, fabric, sanctuary architecture) and the materials used to construct it.
- The content of the work. What do you see? Look at it and notice all the details of the work, such as colors, shapes, figures, and what you understand to be the story being told.
- What the work means. What is it trying to tell you, and why? What does it have to do with God, and the life, work, ministry, and mission of the church?

As congregational leaders gain experience with the arts, they are able to more easily talk together about the relationship between worship and the arts. What art forms would you be comfortable using in worship? What multimedia techniques and methods would best help communicate sermon themes to a worshiping congregation? What multimedia could serve as a medium of God's revealing power, and help provide an experience of God in worship? There are many, many ways to utilize the power of multimedia in worship. What follows are suggestions for viewing and using art, photography, movies, and music in worship.

Using Religious Art and Photography in Worship

For centuries, churches used architecture and stained-glass windows to tell the stories of faith. Beautiful cathedrals like that at Chartres, France, are full of biblical stories in stonework screens and in colored glass. Church artists connected the sacred stories of scripture with the common labors of butchers, bakers, tanners, and the other guilds, reminding the viewer that life is always lived in relationship with God. Other churches hired artists to paint three-paneled wooden altarpieces to tell stories from the Bible. Still others designed and installed mosaics on walls and ceilings to show people the primary stories of scripture.

Today's multimedia technologies provide us a way to show these artistically rendered stories of faith and life. Altarpieces from churches and museums around the world can be shared by projecting their image unto a screen. Images from stained-glass windows, illuminated manuscripts, and oil canvas can now be easily displayed with a computer, a projector, and a screen. Rapid advances in technology put the world's great art at our desktop and with the click of a mouse we can see many works of art digitally reproduced on our computer screen at home, or in our office. Plug a projector into the back of that computer and you can show it on the biggest wall in your house or church, and you will see the full power of the artist's rendering of that familiar gospel story. With a screen, a computer, and a projector, a congregation can experience this artistic interpretation of that story while listening to an oral interpretation of its meaning and power.

Our congregation has seen biblical stories as told by Michelangelo, Caravaggio, van Gogh, Monet, Grunewald, Dali, and Rembrandt. We have also used modern photography to show the work of contemporary artists as they have illustrated life stories and themes that were addressed in worship. A work of art can be displayed during a sermon for a few moments or for the duration of the message. While listening to the sermon, people can see how the story reworked by an artist relates to the message. By referring specifically to an aspect of the work of art during the sermon, the message is experienced by ear and eye. This combining of senses helps gain attention, promotes understanding, and increases retention of your message. Examples of powerful religious art we have used include:

- Matthias Grunewald, *The Crucifixion.* Issenheim Altarpiece (ca. 1515; Musee d'Unterlinden, Colmar, France).

This gruesome depiction of the crucifixion not only helps us see the reality of this cruel death, but it also helps us understand the agony, as well as the hope, in the people gathered at the cross. Mary's hands are clasped in a pleading gesture of prayer, her long fingers extended heavenward. John the Baptist, with a lamb, points his finger up to heaven. The crucified Jesus faces downward. His suffering is real and earthly (he looks down at the earth) and yet it has a connection to God in heaven (through those praying around him).

To understand more about an artwork, it helps to know more of the story surrounding it. Grunewald painted this panel for the chapel of a hospital treating people suffering with a terrible skin disease. In the painting, the skin of the crucified Jesus is covered with the marks of the same disease that was being treated in the hospital. The artist shows those viewing it in the hospital that Jesus knows their pain and suffering. One need not give an art-history lecture as part of a sermon, but by showing this picture, pointing out a few of the details, and offering a story about the painting, it becomes a powerful visual illustration for a sermon.

- Salvador Dali, *The Sacrament of the Last Supper*. (1955; National Gallery of Art, Washington, D.C.).

What is striking about this painting is the transparency of the body of Jesus as he sits at table with the disciples. I showed it as an illustration of the words, "this is my Body," spoken at the Last Supper, to show how the body's transparency reminds us that the world itself is the stage for incarnation and sacrament. Displaying this thought-provoking painting of an event familiar to the worship community serves to stimulate the congregation's imagination. The visual helps them move beyond the actual and literal, and to open them to a new way of seeing.

- Michelangelo Caravaggio, *The Calling of St. Matthew*. (1599–1600; Contarelli Chapel, Church of San Luigi dei Francesi, Rome).

I have already talked about several aspects of this painting, but there is even more to it than what I have mentioned above. Caravaggio shows the moment when Matthew, sitting at the money table with his coworkers, is called to follow Jesus. Jesus, standing in a doorway, points his finger at Matthew, and Matthew, with a quizzical look, seems to be asking, "Who, me?" Within the painting are several scenes and groupings of characters, each of which lends itself to an aspect of what might have happened in the tax office that day. Several people are completely engrossed with the money and are seated in darkness. Next to Matthew is the youngest person in this dark painting, whose face reflects the most light. It is as if the artist is showing in this section of the painting that the hope of the church lies in the youth who are as of yet uncommitted, yet very interested in what is going on. To look carefully at every detail of the painting, and then to read Matthew's Gospel, will reveal that Caravaggio knew the Gospel. Without writing a word, Caravaggio has presented at least nine references to scripture in a single canvas. A scripture-based sermon could be presented with this single visual provided as its backdrop.

Thinking visually can completely transform the way we develop worship. A single image can provide a visual anchor to a theme. If the subject is the parable of the sower, find a picture of a seed, and display the progress of that seed as you describe it in the message. Three little pictures shown during a three-point sermon can make a big difference in helping the message take root in the lives of the hearers. There are many sources of photographic imagery suitable for use in worship. Searchable CD compilations of photographs can be purchased for incorporation into a visual presentation. The Internet has many photographic sites and search engines, but care will need to be exercised so that the imagery is obtained legally. A fine source of photographic imagery is church members themselves.[12]

Every congregation has photographers with hundreds of photographs, slides, videos, and photography equipment. Many church members have video cameras and digital cameras whose images are easily incorporated into a computer. Slides and photographs can be scanned into a computer using standard scanning equipment. An entire team of photographers could be enlisted in a church to take photographs of the church at work and play, as well as to capture any other images within the community. Those with more experience and an eye for what makes good quality photography can be enlisted to train others in the art and skill of photography.

The technical end of this is relatively easy when compared with the bigger challenge of getting us to think visually. Even after years of enjoying photography, art, film, and other visual imagery, I still have to remind myself to think visually when preparing a presentation for church. My word orientation continues to dominate. Many churches already using screens and projection technology are limiting what they show to words of prayers, scriptures, and song lyrics. Many have not yet harnessed the power of imagery to their presentations. Thinking visually takes practice. It means asking, "How can I show what I want to say? What picture will tell the story as well as or better than with words? How can I get that picture? Is there someone I can ask to photograph this image?" One pastor told me, "Our older members were sold on using the screen in worship when, during our prayer concerns, they saw the pictures of their friends who were sick or shut in during the week."[13] Asking members to take pictures of church activities and then editing those images into short presentations can capture the attention of your church, help them understand more of the life and ministry of their church, and stimulate their interest in participating.

Using Movie Clips in Worship

When I tell people that we use videos in church, they generally get a blank look on their faces. When I explain that we find a short, two- to three-minute clip in a movie and show it in worship, they still do not understand. But when I show them the clip and explain in one sentence how I would associate that clip with a sermon theme, they immediately understand. How we use video in worship is something a person has to see . . . but I cannot show you a video clip in this text, so you will have to read through this, maybe find the clip I am referring to, and watch it. How do we find appropriate video scenes? There are many resources available. Several books in the annotated bibliography at the end of this book provide helpful film reviews and a list of some of the theological messages in those films. A number of Web sites provide film clip suggestions indexed by lectionary theme or scriptural text. Michael Rhodes Productions is preparing "Film Clips," a series of scenes from popular films that have been edited for church use and distributed with the permission of the various film companies.[14] A videocassette comes with short clips from three to four different films. A printed guide offers suggestions for how to use the various clips at various points in a worship service, including the call to worship, introduction to the offering, or sermon illustration. My own Web site, www.worshipmedia.com, offers a number of video clip suggestions for use with a variety of specific worship themes and scriptural references.

While resources such as these provide a good start, another source of new material is your own local teams. Watch films together and talk about them using your knowledge of scripture and the human condition to pull out themes and scenes appropriate for use in church. Set them loose as they view home videos, and have them bring suggested scenes to your planning meetings. Prepare worship themes in advance so the team has an idea about the kinds of illustrations and messages they are seeking. As you watch movies for appropriate scenes, remember this: use short segments from the films. Without a license you can use three minutes or less of a single movie.

Although with a license you can show lengthier clips, my experience is that keeping the sequence to a two- to three-minute time length is better. Remember, you are interacting with the media, not letting the media do all the work for you, and you are expecting your congregation to be interacting as well, not getting bored with long, involved dialogues or action that seems to miss the point of your message. A number of resources teach how to watch films with applications for teaching and preaching. I offer here a few of my own suggestions.

- Listen for short, powerful "sermons" in the dialogue.

The *Austin Powers* scene is an example of that, where characters briefly and concisely offer the moral of the story. These short messages leap out at us as summaries of a central theme of the film, or because they speak to our own human condition and need at that particular moment. Worship planners using film will want to look for such scenes with an eye for using them to illustrate a scriptural message some day.

In the film *The Mexican* (2000), a hit man sits with a woman on an airport curb and reflects on the meaning of love. He tells her how, in his experience, people often die afraid, but that those who have experienced love in their lives seem much calmer. This calmness, he says, "comes from the knowledge that somebody somewhere loved them and cared for them and will miss them." We used that scene following the events of September 11, 2001, as a way to illustrate the power that love has to transcend tragedy and death.

In *Pay It Forward* (2000), a teacher challenges his class to think about their lives in relationship to the world. His challenge is simple and to the point, making a perfect scene to show in a worship service that is challenging our sense of mission and purpose: "What does the world expect of you? Nothing. . . . What if the world is just a big disappointment? Unless . . . unless you take the things you don't like about this world and flip them upside down. . . ." On the blackboard is an assignment: "Think of an idea to change our world—and put it into action!"

* Look for references to scripture.

Spider-Man (2002) includes at least three specific biblical quotations as part of its story, including a reciting of the Lord's Prayer in the presence of a scripture-quoting villain. Three or four other scenes in the film compare to familiar biblical stories. In *Pale Rider* (1985) Clint Eastwood's character arrives to save the day just as a passage from Revelation is read. *Titanic* (1997) is full of scriptural references as the ship sinks. The offbeat film *Pi* (1998) features a short commentary by a Hasidic Jew about Hebrew scripture and the numerical and symbolic significance of the Hebrew alphabet. *Rat Race* (2001) follows Matthew 25:35 at the end, along with a clear reference to "the last will be first" in Matthew 20:16. Be on the lookout for obvious theological references. *The Patriot* (2000) opens with a picture of a Bible and a voice talking about "my sin." *Dead Man Walking* (1995) features a conversation about reading the Bible, including the line, "The Bible makes me want to sleep."

The popular *O Brother, Where Art Thou?* (2000) includes a baptism scene where one of the main characters joins a large group of Christians being baptized in a river. As he runs into the water his friend says, "hard times flush the chumps. Everybody's lookin' for answers." The man who runs into the water is baptized while his other friend says, "Delmar's been saved." Delmar returns to his friends, saying, "The preacher done washed away all my sins and transgressions. Neither God nor man's got nothin' on me now. Come on in boys, the water's fine." We used this scene as a call to worship to remind us of our baptism, and that our immersion in worship can be a meaningful, life-changing experience.

In the film *Return to Me* (2000), there is a scene where the main actress is alone at a cafe overlooking Rome, and as the camera pans across the vista, it rests on her. Directly behind her is a cross on a church. The director has situated her perfectly, so the cross is very visible in the background. A waiter, a servant figure, notices the woman's sadness and she begins to explain her mood. "I'll take my break now," he says, as he sits to listen, a generous, compassionate, and merciful gesture, provided in the presence of the cross of Christ. The cross in the background offers a silent blessing at this moment of compassionate caring for another person.

Watch for ways that scriptural theme is reshaped to fit a film's purpose. *The Matrix* (1999) refers to the web of sin in human life with references to birth, baptism, a John the Baptist figure, and an awaited Messiah. The typologies fit nicely except for one thing: the messianic figure takes up weapons and uses violence to settle the problem. We know the Messiah takes up the cross and the road of nonviolence to show Love's power. The film offers a way to compare and contrast its story with that of our faith story.

• Pay attention to the art, literature, and music that is used in a film.

Absolute Power (1997) opens with a scene in the National Gallery in Washington, D.C., that features a close-up view of a face painted on a canvas. Soon the camera shows the entire painting: St. Francis receiving the stigmata. Why does that open the film? What does the story of St. Francis receiving the stigmata have to do with the main character in the film? As the story unfolds and you reflect back upon the meaning of the painting, you will understand how, like Francis, the film's main character sees something that changes him, and like Francis, reverses his course in life. By studying the painting and the story to which it refers, you will find a way to interpret the entire film. We used this scene to open a Lenten program about the life and ministry of St. Francis, and to show his continuing influence upon modern art and culture.

In *City of Joy* (1992) there is a scene that features a painting hanging above a couch. Later, as the character moves to another apartment, the painting is carried out of the apartment and we get a better look at it. It is Gericault's *The Raft of the Medusa*, in which a group of shipwrecked people are lying on a raft in a stormy sea in various states of death, despair, and hopelessness. A handful of people on the edge of the raft and facing the horizon begin to show great hope as they see a ship in the distance. They wave rags of clothing to call attention to their plight. The film, set in modern India, uses the painting to refer to the underlying theme of hope out of hopelessness.

If a novel, a play, or a poem is mentioned, go to those works and read them later to find the deeper meaning of the film. In *The Pledge* (2001), there is a reference to a Hans Christian Andersen poem. By reading this text, a viewer confused by the film's ending might be able to understand it better.

The soundtrack presents an opportunity to learn how filmmakers link music with their images (a feature of electronic language). Notice what songs are played and how they fit the movie's story. A full listing of all the music used in a film is available when the credits roll. Some film soundtrack collections become greatly popular with the listening audience and provide easy access to some of the striking music in a film. Pay particular attention to the song played over the credits, because it often summarizes the filmmaker's primary message. For example, in *Magnolia* (1999) the credits were shown to a haunting plea for salvation in Amie Mann's "Save Me." In *Original Sin* (2001) the moviegoer is left with the message, "Don't Give Up On Love."

- More film viewing suggestions

Watch for cross symbolism. For some reason, Hollywood is filling the screen with depictions of the cross at "crucial" scenes. It is customary for directors to add one or two crosses in a window or door to signal that one or two persons will be sacrificed during the film, or to signal a turning point in the film. I asked a Hollywood screenwriter if the cross references are deliberate in today's films, and he said, "definitely." When the soldiers decide to make their final stand in *Saving Private Ryan* (1998), a telephone pole-cross is fixed in the center of the frame. *Sense and Sensibility* (1995) closes a nighttime vigil at the bedside of a gravely ill young woman with a morning view of a cross-shaped garden outside her window. The resolution to the crisis follows. The final episode of the TV show *The X-Files* closed with a close-up shot of a small silver cross resting on the finger of an actor as he speaks the words, "Maybe there's hope."

Pay attention to small details. Films often cost $1,000,000 a minute to produce, which figures out to $16,666 per second. Nothing is put into that film accidentally. Little details, like numbers on license plates, apartment doors, home addresses, and the time on clocks, can have additional meaning. Directors sometimes pick random numbers, but often will add some symbolic meaning. For example, in an early scene of *The Pledge*, we see Jack Nicholson's license-plate numbers, and they add up to 13, foreshadowing the bad luck that will come to him. David Bruce at www.hollywoodjesus.com offers more such number symbolism in his review of the film *Unbreakable* (2000), which addresses issues of good and evil. In *Rules of Engagement* (2000), the very large clock in the courtroom reads 11:11 at the start of testimony in the court-martial of the main character—numbers that mean a lot to veterans, November 11, Armistice Day. Color is another symbolic detail. Stanley Kubrick's *Eyes Wide Shut* (1999), a morality play about fidelity in marriage, presents brilliantly juxtaposed colors. The use of primary colors, greens, reds, and yellows, is obvious. The film shows the characters struggling to live out life's primary values.

Practicing these and other film viewing techniques can help you and your team watch enjoyable films while appreciating their connection to the goals of the worship and the learning settings of the church. With the use of a video capture program, available through many computer software companies, and a VHS or DVD machine plugged into a computer, short film clips may be copied and edited from movies that have been legally obtained by an individual, imported into a presentation program, and then shown. A single copy of the segment, no more than 10 percent or three minutes of a film, may be made from a legally obtained copy of the film as long as proper credit is displayed. Using this same software, it is possible to create your own film scenes by editing together a number of short video clips. A member of our production team put together images from denominational mission videos to the Joan Osborne song, "One of Us," in which the singer raises the implications of the incarnation with her question, "What if God was one of us?" While the song was used in another fashion on two other occasions, this was the first time a song was used as a soundtrack for a sequence of mission video clips. Our team member reviewed our church's collection of mission videotapes and a purchased copy of a video featuring the face of Jesus in art. She edited the clips together and fit them to the lyrics of the song. This four-minute multimedia production illustrated how we are the Body of Christ in the world.

Using Music with Art

In 1973, I worked with a group of seminary friends to publish *A Media Sourcebook,*[15] and in it we listed contemporary music that we thought could stimulate discussion in a church educational setting, or illustrate a worship theme. We listed meaningful songs from popular, folk, and folk-rock musical styles, and grouped them into categories like "movement songs," "social protest and musical statements about our society," "loneliness, frustration, helplessness," "the wheel of life/spiritual," "statements about the earth," "theological or philosophical statement," and "albums worth experiencing." We included over 500 songs. As I look at that list 30 years later, I see that much of the music could be used in today's church. What was on the edge then has become mainstream today. Many clergy during those years (and most clergy serving churches today were trained in the 1960s and '70s) learned how to put slides to music, and did so with as many as eight slide projectors simultaneously. The combination of emotionally powerful imagery with the beat, rhythm, melody, and lyric of the music demonstrated the power of multimedia.[16]

What happened? If clergy knew the power of music in those years, and learned how to connect images to that music, how come so few clergy and churches continued to develop this art form over the years? If my own story is any indicator, it was the unspoken rule that the oral arts of liturgy, preaching, and organ-accompanied music is the appropriate worship standard. As Leonard Sweet has observed, we were "culturally circumcised,"[17] that is, initiated into the rule and practice of print-oriented, wordy worship. To bring so-called secular music into the church is for some a big step to take. Many churches allow only sacred music in the sanctuary, which is narrowly defined as classical music or more-recent compositions with overtly religious language (like the tremendously popular "In the Garden" and "How Great Thou Art").

Churches trying to be culturally relevant have begun to include praise music in their liturgies. Using simple, repetitive choruses, such music is easily learned and comfortably sung. Many churches are experimenting with other musical traditions and opening up their tradition to include spirituals, jazz, blues, polkas, and Christian rock. Within today's congregations are a variety of musical tastes. Asking church members about the radio stations they listen to and about what they have included in their personal collections will give an idea of the kinds of music they prefer. Why not bring to the worship setting the music people listen to in daily life? Martin Luther incorporated tavern tunes as he rewrote lyrics. There is good tradition for using music of our times and turning it towards praise, thanksgiving, and teaching. Presenting the music a congregation listens to at home and work in the worship setting captures attention, and with the addition of imagery, can lead to a fresh understanding of God's word in relationship to human life.

Whenever possible, I prefer to have our own musicians prepare songs that they like to play and sing. That said, adding music that has been professionally recorded adds another dimension to worship, especially considering the professional quality of such a song. The artistic twist that our multimedia worship team brings to such music is illustrating the music with art and photography. By adding the visuals, we are able to make the song a part of the theme presentation in a way that just playing the song does not accomplish. Combining pictures with music brings a powerful message, because the more senses we touch, the more likely we are to affect both thoughts and feelings of worshipers, and the more likely they are to be touched by God. Those church members who volunteer to provide a song for our multimedia service are given the scriptural theme of the worship service and a brief description of how the song fits that theme. Their job is to find pictures that they think illustrate the song and the scriptural theme. These volunteers are religious artists in the sense that they are interpreting scripture through music and imagery. What they develop is then experienced by the worshiping congregation, and they too are invited into the process of experiencing a word from God through music and imagery.

This creative process extends to film too. We have sometimes played a film clip and added a different soundtrack to it by turning down the film sound and playing a song. This effectively creates a new soundtrack that brings the imagery and music in line with a sermon theme. For example, one of our media team put together sequences from the film *Jesus of Nazareth* (1997) that illustrated the betrayal, arrest, procession with the cross, and crucifixion. She played the haunting song "Angel" by Sarah McLachlan as these clips were shown. We used this particular media piece to conclude a Maundy Thursday worship service in the worship sanctuary. People left in silence, visibly moved by this dramatic summary of the events of the latter part of Maundy Thursday and Good Friday.

As with film and art, there are a number of songs with obvious religious references. The 1960s song "Turn, Turn, Turn" by the Byrds uses verses from Ecclesiastes. The 1990s brought "A Christmas Song" by Dave

Matthews with references to the annunciation, nativity, life, and teachings of Jesus, as well as a retelling of the story of the Last Supper and crucifixion. "When Love Comes to Town" by U2 and B. B. King is a song about sin and salvation. Thousands of other songs raise the same issues that are addressed in many sermons: faithfulness, loyalty, doubt, forgiveness, sinfulness, brokenness, death, dying, life's meaning, love, sex, and marriage.

Using the Language

Using electronic language in worship takes some practice. Here is a little exercise you can do alone, or with a small team, to practice finding multimedia suitable to illustrate a religious theme.

- Select a favorite biblical text.
- Determine the theme you wish to draw out of the text.
- Practice using musical language by finding music you think expresses your theme with a minimum of explanation.
- List two or three songs or pieces of music that communicate your theme, and decide what order you would play them.
- Get the songs and play them.
- Played in sequence, do they communicate the theme you have selected? What did you think about as you listened to the music in relationship to the theme? How did the musical language effectively get your message across? What did you think was missing?
- Think about adding visuals to accompany the music. List some images you would use to illustrate both your theme, and the music you have selected. What art could you use? What pictures would you ask someone to draw? What photographs might you take? What symbols would you show?
- If you have 35 mm slides, or a computer, put together a slide show of images to illustrate your songs.
  — Find out the length of the song and calculate the length of the song in seconds.
  — Decide the amount of time you would like most pictures to be shown, anywhere from 5 to 15 seconds. If you figured on 10 seconds per slide, you would show around 20 slides in the course of a song that lasts around three minutes.
- Watch your program on your computer or with a slide projector as you

play your music. How does the imagery you have selected add to the power of the song? What does the imagery take away?

- Next, think of two or three movie scenes you think could illustrate your theme. What do you remember about those scenes?

- If you can find those movies in a video store or public library, locate the scenes and look at them. How well do they fit your theme? What would you have to say to introduce these scenes in order to relate them to your theme? What might you say after the scene has been shown?

- If you have come this far, you have assembled some materials for a multimedia presentation of your scriptural theme. What is your best lineup for the material? How could you organize your three songs and two video clips to best communicate your theme?

- Present your multimedia reflection to a group in your congregation. With a slide projector, CD player, and a VCR hooked to a TV, you can show what you have created. How would you orally introduce your media, and what would you say in between segments to highlight and describe your theme?

A next step would be to get a confirmation class or youth group to work with you on a similar process. Or, identify people in your church that you know love music, watch videos or go to movies, appreciate the visual arts, use photography, know about computer presentation software, or are just excited about new worship forms, and invite them to join with you to produce a vesper program or sample worship experience using multimedia.

Jesus taught with parables in the language of his time, which was the oral culture of storytelling. He took situations from daily life and turned them into metaphors about God's kingdom. When we incorporate into worship the parables of the electronic age found in film, art, photography, and music, we too can turn these into metaphors about God's reign. Through these media, worship leaders and artists tell something about faith using the languages of our time: print, oral, and electronic.

In the next chapter, we will look at some practical considerations associated with developing multimedia worship, including the need for work teams, guidelines for using media, paying attention to copyright law, and assembling the technical equipment you will want to use.

CHAPTER 4

Producing Multimedia Worship

In this chapter we will look at some of the practical issues associated with multimedia worship, including the need to:

- enlist and train a number of work teams that contribute to the development and production process of your multimedia materials
- develop production guidelines for your congregation's multimedia presentations
- understand U.S. copyright law in relationship to the multimedia you use
- secure the equipment you will need to produce and present multimedia worship

Creative Teamwork

Producing multimedia worship is a team sport that involves the contribution of many hands and minds. I quickly learned that it is silly, and stress producing, for one person to try to do all the tasks associated with multimedia. When showing the mission videos mentioned in an earlier chapter, I walked to the television set, turned it on, adjusted the microphone, turned on the videotape machine, adjusted volumes and brightness, and then stood there as the congregation watched the short video clip. Then I turned off the TV set, walked back to the pulpit, and talked about what we had just seen. I remember how awkward this was, and I felt all the stress of wondering whether the equipment would work and if people would be able to see and hear the program. I realized then, "I cannot do this alone." Adding multimedia to our worship life has helped me become a better team player in my congregation. Where I once thought I needed to know how to do everything in a church, and took great pleasure in learning different tasks, I have learned that other church members like to join in the fun too. Many of them love to share their gifts and skills, and are willing to devote hours of their free time to make a significant contribution to the life of their church. As we developed multimedia worship in our church, I became determined to grow a process where the church would depend upon its members to produce and lead its multimedia worship services.

Leaders planning to use multimedia in worship will want to identify and enlist people who have varieties of interests and gifts. Enlist large numbers of people who want to share their unique talents. It is an opportunity to invite into this work a church's artists, photographers, musicians, computer operators, projectionists, organizers, enlisters, theologians, film buffs, and music appreciators. In case you wonder where you find them, start with the small group of people who are committed to and share the vision. Bill Easum says the way to find people is to share the vision of what you want to do, and then "watch whose eyes light up."[1] Those who join with you will grow in their excitement and bring in other friends and family members to join in the fun.

Early in our own process of adding a media-intensive worship service to our Sunday morning schedule, our church council authorized a request for a small grant through a regional denominational office. The grant allowed us to hire two individuals to work part time to recruit persons to help develop a multimedia service that would begin in the fall of that year. They looked for those with computer skills, ability to work with sound systems, and interest in video and music. The two women who were hired to do this work came from within our congregation, had an interest in multimedia worship, and were able to work eight hours a week to recruit volunteers and to assist me in planning and creating our additional worship service. They also kept contact with people who made commitments to produce various media for our services.

After nine months, enough people were involved on a voluntary basis that we no longer needed to hire individuals for this work. A lively energy developed as dozens of people joined small working groups. People who were inactive or "sleeper" members became more actively involved because we asked them to share their technical skills and gifts. Members who had neither the time nor inclination to serve on a church committee stepped forward to give even more time to our worship leadership tasks. These people invited others to come to worship because they found our multimedia worship service to be so different and so powerful. They invited friends and family to what they experienced as a meaning-rich environment. They were excited that in worship they could experience faith interpreted by the real life of film and popular music.

As more and more people became involved, they came to "own" the whole concept of multimedia worship, and it was no longer a special project of a single vision committee or a single pastor, but a part of the web of life of the whole congregation. Everyone had a stake in what was happening. Opportunities for service multiplied through the church. We encouraged people to develop and share their gifts. People came to church and received training from other church members on how to use computers. Adults and youth set up appointments with one another to learn software like Microsoft PowerPoint using church facilities and donated equipment. Youth who did not have computers or Internet at home were invited to come to church and work with their friends on church-related projects. Several youth fulfilled community service requirements by putting in hours developing media projects for worship services. Some church members upgraded their home computer equipment so they could better produce multimedia programs for church from their homes.

There are a number of ways that church members can contribute to the development of multimedia worship. People may be organized into special interest groups that contribute to developing multimedia worship. Their different interests and perspectives contribute directly and indirectly to multimedia production. Some of these groups might meet weekly, while others meet less frequently. While each kind of group may have a unique interest or function, they may be brought in as resources for your multimedia planning at any time.

Dreamers

Multimedia worship best flows out of the core values of a forward-looking congregation. One way for a church to stay in touch with those core values while stimulating forward progress is to encourage a group of people to regularly discuss the future. This long-range planning group, responsible to your governing board, can involve a number of people who are reading, talking, learning, and planning together. While this group is not directly involved with producing multimedia worship, the energy they create as they learn and think together radiates outward to affect the entire congregation. As they communicate their plans and ideas with other committees, boards, working groups, and social groups within a church, everyone learns and grows. They gradually contribute to a growing congregational awareness that ongoing learning and discussion are helping to create a climate for innovation. This group helps the whole congregation understand the issues they are discussing, and why, by keeping the whole church informed through verbal reports, bulletin inserts, and newsletter articles. Other small groups may be enlisted to learn more about how to incorporate multimedia into worship. These may be organized around specific interest areas such as those described below.

Techies

Most churches have people who are able to serve as technical advisers. These are the techies of your church who love to learn and talk about multimedia equipment such as computers, projectors, screens, videotape machines, video recorders, digital cameras, sound equipment like microphones, speakers, and amplifiers, and all the other gadgets they may already be using at home, school, or at work. This group may be asked to investigate what worship technologies and equipment other churches are using, and take an inventory of the technical equipment your church already has. They may develop a list of the immediate, essential items your church will need to further its multimedia production and presentation capabilities, as well as a wish list of items your church may want to add in the future. This group could start by disposing outdated film projectors, stereos, and other clutter found in many church closets and basements. More importantly, they can keep the church's worship technologies updated, may help troubleshoot problems, and can assist in training church members how to use equipment properly and more efficiently.

Film Buffs

This group of people is made of those who watch lots of movies in theaters and at home. It is a group you will turn to when you are looking for video illustrations of worship themes. They learn how to talk about film from a faith perspective, and begin to see scenes that could relate to particular worship themes. Members of this group might watch a film together at the theater, go to a cafe afterwards, and talk about the story, characters, and theological issues raised by the film. They might also talk together about a recent worship service and whether there was something in the film that might have related to the scripture or topic that was addressed. These people may be asked to practice their viewing skills when they watch movies at home, and to find scenes from the films they watch that might relate to coming worship themes. Scenes they might watch for include a character struggling to understand the meaning of life, or applying faith to a situation. Some might want to keep a notebook for future reference, including a list of the films they have seen and the location of important scenes in the film. DVD viewers can list the chapter, hour, and minute of important sequences. VHS watchers can check for the hour and minute of the sequence, but will need to be sure to have started the movie at 0:00 on their counter. When the group next comes together to view scenes from films, it may be helpful to reinforce the idea that it is possible to watch films for pleasure while keeping religious applications in mind.

Music Lovers

Every congregation includes people who listen to a wide variety of musical styles. An invitation could be extended to church members to bring to a meeting samples of favorite music they think relate to their faith in some way. It is helpful to have them bring along the lyrics to the songs either on the CD-liner notes or from the Internet. Having the lyrics helps to know more about what the song is about and whether in fact it does fit a worship purpose. At this gathering, group members could listen to the music and begin to relate it to various worship themes. These discussions give people permission to relate their music to the worship setting and will get them listening to their music in new ways. They could be asked to come up with music ideas for future worship themes.

Artists

The photographers, artists, and art educators in a congregation could be invited to a session at church to talk about posters, prints, slides, and other imagery that could be used to communicate a particular worship theme.

These people could be encouraged to look at art and photography with an eye for what religious themes these materials might help develop. What would they show the congregation to illustrate a particular scripture reading? They could be invited to bring samples of their own work. The group could talk together about how they might assist others in the congregation to learn basic skills such as taking photographs with a digital camera at church, or making a video of church events. Perhaps they would be willing to help organize field trips for church members to visit art museums and special exhibits, and help lead a discussion about what they have seen.

As a way to generate ideas for future uses of multimedia in worship, members of these various small groups could come together to talk about how to bring their favorite multimedia art into the worship life of the church. A month's worth of coming worship service themes could be presented to them. They might look at lectionary passages, scriptural topics, contemporary themes, or a sermon series, and brainstorm the kinds of media that could illustrate the material. After reading scripture together and discussing a focusing theme, the group could list specific media that could be used to illustrate that theme.

Planning Process

The team process in the congregation I serve includes an annual gathering where themes and topics for the coming worship year are suggested, discussed, and developed. Those who come to this gathering are asked to bring their ideas, along with any ideas they have solicited from other church members at committee meetings or other gatherings. The congregation is regularly asked to provide worship topics and theme ideas. The Christian education committee is asked to share their curriculum plan for the coming year, since worship themes might be coordinated to coincide with certain lessons. Those who come to the planning session take a look at the lectionary cycle as well as the seasons of the church year. The goal of this planning session, and any follow-up sessions, is to develop a worship plan for the September through May worship cycle of Sundays. (Presently we give a summer sabbatical to the media teams. Occasional media productions are developed and used in summer worship as the Spirit moves.) Once future themes and topics are determined, they are assigned to specific weeks and months of the coming year. This scheduling is sometimes done during the planning meeting, but most often at another planning session with those who will take most responsibility for developing the worship themes, including the clergy and any other interested team members. This schedule is typed and given to all interested in continuing with the planning process throughout the year. Those interested in developing multimedia worship then know the themes and topics as well as the time of year when they will be presented.

Occasionally, we extend invitations to the congregation to join in a special seasonal planning session to brainstorm worship themes and media enhancements for, as an example, Advent through Christmas. This session serves the multiple purpose of gathering people to study the meaning of a particular church season, to read scripture together, and to focus attention on themes and topics which would best communicate the season to the congregation during worship. Another strength of this process is that it brings together people who listen to a wide variety of music and who may watch a number of movies. This expands the repertoire of music and film a congregation might use, and helps us relate to the wider variety of musical tastes within a congregation. New people continue to be incorporated into this widely shared process, and suddenly worship planning and development no longer become clergy-centered, but an integral part of an entire congregation's life.

Weekly Worship

In the congregation I serve, a core working group of three to five volunteers works closely with me on a weekly, and sometimes daily, basis to develop our media-intensive worship service. These are the individuals who have committed themselves to developing our multimedia worship on a regular basis. They most likely will have attended the annual planning session and any subsequent scheduling meetings. They have the time, energy, and inclinations needed to provide worship on a weekly basis.

A typical weekly production session begins within the context of all of the planning that has gone before: the setting of the worship calendar and the topical, scriptural, or seasonal themes; monthly meetings to focus on the next four or five Sundays; and any listing of songs or film clips that might be used in the future. The core team gathers on a Monday evening to plan for the following Sunday. The worship leader lays out the worship theme and scriptural focus, and briefly outlines the direction the sermon message will take. The team brainstorms songs and film clips that might relate to this message. Since they have known the general topic for weeks in advance, the team has already generated lists of songs and film clips that may relate to the coming themes. On this night, the group will listen to songs and look at lyrics, as well as preview potential film clips. As decisions are made about which songs to use, a team member is assigned the task of finding visual illustrations to be shown as the song is played during worship. Sometimes a member of the congregation will have already offered to provide a song, and the team previews this and any accompanying visual illustrations to determine whether the piece fits the service theme. The team makes suggestions for additional service music, including any hymns or songs. They give input on whether hymnals will be used or lyrics projected on the screen, and sometimes help contact any musicians that are needed. Film clips are previewed and a decision is made about where to start and end the scene, knowing that the clip will be no more than three minutes. There is additional discussion about any other visual illustrations that will need to be prepared, including scripture text, prayers, and sermon illustrations, as well as any additional pictures or imagery that might be displayed while the preacher is presenting the message. This meeting lasts anywhere from one to two hours.

During the week, team members are busy with their tasks. By Friday morning, any service announcements, prayers, and scripture texts are typed into the computer in the sanctuary. Someone in the church office or a volunteer does this. Songs and visuals may be reviewed with the preacher at any time during the week. Members of the team who will work the equipment on Sunday morning will meet at some point on Friday or Saturday to make sure all is ready. During this session we review film clips, music, and all imagery. We decide the final order of presentation based upon the flow of the presenter's message. This meeting may take as long as two hours. There may be last-minute adjustments during the worship service itself. The presenter may decide against showing a song or film clip because of time constraints or a shift in the focus of the message. The presenting team running the equipment needs only to be notified of this fact and the worship moves ahead seamlessly with little visual interruption. We have learned to use blank, colored slides between media illustrations as a way to allow for any changes. It is possible for the computer operator to leapfrog over a film clip or complete song in a PowerPoint presentation, for example, by going to the blue screen on the projector. With the touch of a button, the congregation sees a blue-colored screen while the computer person moves ahead to the desired slide. Those churches using two computers and proper switches can make adjustments even more swiftly.

While it is possible to provide multimedia worship with a single person running the computer and projector, it is advisable to have at least one other person assisting. Another set of hands is always welcomed to help run the projector, computer, video and CD machine, and set volume levels. The team will know their comfort levels. Some services may be accomplished with one person, while others with more complex media may require an additional person or two. As a team gains experience working together, they will gain comfort with working equipment together. They will want to regularly consult about their schedules, since it is difficult to expect volunteers to be present week after week.

Back-up technicians who know how to run the projector and computer further support the core team in our congregation. It is possible to schedule this assistance in advance. Additional working groups of varying sizes are also involved for differing periods of time. These people may scan images into a computer and take photographs with digital cameras that are later imported into the computer software. They may search the Internet and find images to illustrate songs that have been selected around a particular theme. They may work with a home computer to capture short video scenes that will be used in the future, or type written material such as quotations or scripture texts into slides for use in a worship service. Some may devote their skills on a monthly basis while others work less frequently, or, as they are inspired. In our experience, as various church people and visitors notice the artistic efforts of all of these people, they offer their own suggestions of songs and films, and sometimes offer to participate in a creative effort. Often they ask for the training to help them do so. The entire church is energized by the new skills released into the life of the congregation.

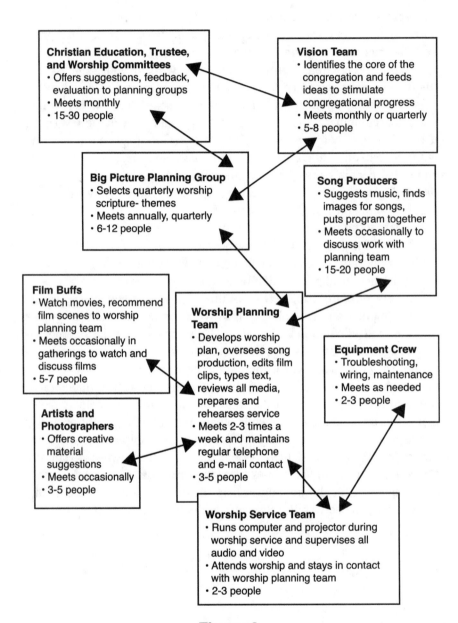

Figure 2

Diagram of a team planning process

Language Matters

Each worship community already has in place its own rules, guidelines, and standards regarding what topics are acceptable for discussion, and what music, language, and behavior are permitted. Many of these guidelines may be unspoken, yet implicitly in place. For example, some communities expect the clergy will always preach from behind the pulpit. Other communities expect only traditional hymns will be used. Clergy understand that certain words or off-hand expressions might be unacceptable during a sermon. As worship teams develop multimedia worship, they will want to identify the guidelines already operative within the church, and think about what may or may not be different as multimedia is introduced.

Most worship teams have agreed that someone has final authority over what is seen and heard in worship, and this authority generally rests with the clergyperson responsible for the service. This is where the buck stops. It may already be clear to everyone that the responsible clergy has the right of editorial control, and enforces all standards and guidelines agreed upon by others involved in worship planning and leadership. If this is not clear, then all interested parties will need to decide where the final authority and responsibility for worship resides. Many worship teams already have a style of collaborative planning and leadership that encourages team members to communicate clearly with one another. The entire worship planning process requires that people learn to talk together, share ideas freely, address their feelings and disagreements when they come, and move on quickly and effectively. It requires constantly reminding one another of the role and purpose of worship, and of the worship team's responsibility to communicate the Word of God in worship.

The issues worship teams already deal with on a weekly basis are quite similar to those they will address when planning multimedia worship services. There are some guidelines, however, that may be unique to multimedia worship and that multimedia teams will want to consider. Some of the guidelines our worship team works with are:

Source of Material. This issue concerns whether we will only use religious resources in worship, or will use material from popular culture. There are plenty of films with religious content that can be used in worship. The films about Jesus all have scenes that could be used in worship, including references to parables, scripture, and biblical themes. There is a whole genre of Christian musical recordings that could be played during the worship service. Then there is the vast library of films and songs from popular culture that also can serve to illustrate worship topics and themes. You and your teams will want to have a discussion about your standards concerning the source of audiovisual materials you will use in worship.

Imagery. Our church is located in a predominantly white community with little ethnic diversity. We therefore deliberately include multicultural imagery in the art and photography we use as a way to remind ourselves that we live in a world larger than our small locality. Another issue associated with imagery is that of nudity. Our team has decided it would be against the standards of the congregation to show nudity in a film clip. On one occasion, however, we showed a clip from the film *Jesus of Nazareth* (1997), in which a naked demoniac fled from Jesus. Since it was faithful to the scriptural text, a rear view, and on screen for less than a second, the team thought it appropriate. A church member mentioned the scene to the team a few days later and asked if it were appropriate. The team's defense was that it was what the scripture said had happened. The man was naked in the story. You will have to make your own judgment on such things. Our team also has had to decide whether to use scenes depicting sexual encounters. Worship standards in various communities may differ from place to place. Our team elects not to show sexual material in order not to risk distressing members of the congregation. An important consideration for all teams is whether the emotional impact of any scene may be so powerful as to distract the congregation from the direction of your message. This standard is appropriate for violent imagery. When a violent scene helps you deliver your message, what level of violence will you tolerate? What kind of violence will you allow, and how graphic? With so many films using violence or the threat of violence to tell their story, and with church people rightly concerned about such violence in our media, what will be your team's approach? We discuss this frequently, and have decided not to portray violent acts, although on occasion we have shown characters agonizing over the reality of violence or its threat.

Artistic Edge. While we might want to include only lovely, beautiful art in worship, one of our standards is to watch for imagery that has an edge to it, the edge of real life that includes sin, trial, and death. We think it important to provide imagery that leads us to greater awareness of both the promise and the reality of faith and doubt, of hope and struggle, of joy and sadness, of cross and empty tomb. Another edge is to recognize that pictures that literally represent a song lyric limit the imagination of the viewer, while something less representational offers a more open interpretation that stimulates more interaction between the viewer and what is seen.

Language. We avoid video clips and songs that include offensive language. Even the terms *hell* and *damn* are avoided unless we warn of their presence and perhaps offer a reason why we have chosen to include them. When we have allowed those words, it has been because our media team has felt they help communicate the theological meaning we are drawing out of the scene. Mostly, however, video-editing equipment allows us to delete offensive language. On rare occasions we have simply turned the volume down. (Once we "planted" a team member in the sanctuary who started to cough loudly as the "bad word" was delivered on screen!)

Slide Readability Guidelines. It is important that computer-generated slides be visible and clear. There are many choices of background colors, text color and size, animation of words, and word positioning. The communication goal is to make the slides and the information they contain readable and understandable from various distances and locations in a worship space. These standards will vary according to the size of your screen and your sanctuary. The last pews in our sanctuary are 50 feet from the screen. The guidelines we give those who are producing materials for our church are:[2]

- keep all text and pictures at least one inch from the top of the slide, since the top of the slide is sometimes cut off on the screen
- leave a small margin on the other three sides, since the screen is not perfectly square
- use a font size of 40 or larger
- use simple, bold fonts that are easy to read
- add a shadow effect to help the text stand out more
- use contrasting colors for text (white and yellow are often the best)
- fill as much of the slide as you can, either with text or a picture

Length and Number of Video Clips and Songs. We keep all video to under three minutes in order to follow copyright law (see below) and the "laws" of attention span. Showing too much video, just like reading an overly long quotation, can lose the attention of the viewer or listener. We monitor songs for length as well, and we sometimes fade them out after the main point has been made. We generally use a combination of four or five media for a 35-minute worship experience. Three video clips (with a maximum of four) seem to be just the right amount of video in a service, and we generally use only two songs along with visual imagery. Too many images can create visual overload.

Continuity. In radio and TV, the term *dead air* is used to describe the unacceptable silence that sometimes occurs when, unintentionally, no sound is broadcast. Radio and TV program directors know that in their business, sound is essential at all times. In worship, dead air is an unintended silent interval that sometimes happens between events. I am not talking here about intentional silence, and the pregnant pause after a particularly moving story or media illustration. I am referring to the uncomfortable silences that may result from poor preparation, missed signals with a technical team, or equipment glitches. These unplanned intervals (for example, a videotape or DVD not cued properly, a wrong song number pressed on a CD player, poor volume level, the computer freezing up, or poor communication within the worship team) can interrupt the flow of worship. Yet these things happen. I try to have a story ready when we need some time for a technical adjustment. I once talked about an experience at a grocery store when all the computers unexpectedly shut down and the cashiers started manually entering prices. I spoke of how some people lost their patience and stormed out of the store, while others used the time to talk together. Patience is a good thing to have, I said, when working with technology. This little interlude provided the time our technicians needed to fix their problem, and it kept the congregation engaged. Sometimes you will need to just move on to the next point while the technicians do what they need to do. Take a cue from radio and television: when the tape they are describing does not play, the announcer provides a verbal summary of what was to be seen or heard. Learn from the mistakes and go on from there.

Just because churches might have guidelines in place does not mean that they are always followed. What happens when guidelines are tested and challenged? Our multimedia worship team has had to discuss several situations that stretched our limits. We used a scene from the movie *Wall Street* (1987) to illustrate the commandment not to steal. We were aware that near the particular scene, an inappropriate swearword was used. We carefully cued the video so it would start after that word had been used, but the tape backed itself up when the power on the machine was turned on, and, since we did not know this had happened, the word slipped out. I did not comment at the time, but later that day team members and I received calls from people asking one question: "Did you mean to allow that word out, or was it an accident?" They were satisfied that it was an accident, but it did remind us of the high level of vigilance required in the worship setting. As the team supervisor, I apologized to the congregation the next week and reiterated our standards for the use of media in our service. Members of the congregation responded by saying, "Don't let that one mistake stop you from using relevant and powerful material."

On another occasion, a team member put together pictures to accompany the John Mellencamp song, "Your Life Is Now." In the lyric is the question, "Would you teach your children to tell the truth?" The woman selecting imagery for the song used a picture of the White House for those lyrics. This was during the controversy over whether President Clinton was being truthful in his statements about Monica Lewinsky. I asked that the image be changed because it seemed that the emotional power of the White House imagery at that particular date would detract not only from the overall message the song developed, but would also swing the message from the sermon theme the song served to illustrate.

While previewing the imagery another team member used to illustrate a song, I noticed that all of the people portrayed were white. I simply stated that I felt it important to portray more of the diversity of all of God's people in our imagery, since we are members of a diverse human family. The message was heard and team members have become more aware of the need to portray diversity in areas such as race, sex, physical condition, age, and social class.

All of America was glued to the television screen in the days following the terror attack on New York, Washington, and Pennsylvania. We watched the media develop montages of moving and still pictures of the tragedy, its human toll, and its heroes while playing soundtracks of patriotic or religious music. Some of my production team members were influenced by this and wanted to do the same in worship the following Sunday. This impulse on their part came from a need to creatively express their own feelings with the worship community, and to offer that community a faith-based interpretation of this experience. My struggle was to be faithful to the worship message and to calm the emotions of a people already exposed to a large number of mass-media and audiovisual presentations.

Because I felt the church need not duplicate the patriotic music or imagery theme, I asked that we not show pictures of the tragedy; rather, end with the song "For the Love of It All" by Peter, Paul and Mary, using imagery which led us to continue to place our trust in God. The song is a marvelous telling of the work of Love at the creation, the fall, the birth and crucifixion of Jesus, and how "it is still not too late to come celebrate the Love of it all." After a good discussion of this on Saturday night, my production team agreed. But between that conversation and Sunday morning, they just could not resist putting together a dozen images to "Amazing Grace" and asked me on Sunday morning if they could close the service with that production. I reluctantly agreed since I did not have the time or energy to discuss again what we had talked about the previous day, and since I wanted to honor the creative and theological sense of my team. I told them, however, that we would evaluate it during the week.

They showed their production, and it seemed to me to be just what NBC or other networks had been doing all week, bagpipes included. Members left the service teary-eyed and reporting the final song and its imagery to be the high point of the service. Yet for me, what happened was that the closing changed the emphasis of the service away from affirmation of God's abiding love and towards the theme that even though we are saddened by the attack, we shall be strong together as an American people. At a minimum, this illustrates how worship and worship leadership changes when we clergy invite laity into our "sacred sanctum" and give them permission to be leaders and ministers in their own right.

Within any group responsible for leading worship, there will be a variety of theological perspectives and different levels of education and sophistication. Clergy leaders will want to continually articulate their own theological views, explain them, and relate them to the theological framework of the congregation, while seeking to understand the views of the others with whom they work.

There are many production guidelines that congregations will consider and work with as they learn to develop multimedia worship resources.

Concerning Copyright

In this section, we take a careful look at one of the most important production guidelines worship leaders will want to address, that of learning about and applying U.S. copyright law to their situation.

"What about copyright?" is often the first question people ask when considering how to incorporate multimedia into services of worship. It is a good question because it shows legal and ethical awareness. Copyright law clarifies the rights and responsibilities of those who create original works, and those who wish to use these works as they continue a creative process. Churches, like everyone else, must comply with U.S. law. While not a roadblock to the use of multimedia in worship, U.S. copyright law is a speed bump that forces us to slow down and think about how we will legally and ethically use copyrighted material. If churches are going to celebrate and utilize the creativity of a wide variety of artists, we must be willing to do so carefully and ethically. Using multimedia in our worship demands a conscientious, intentional approach to the use of copyrighted material.

Licenses

Several companies sell blanket licenses to churches so they may legally use certain materials in a wide variety of church settings.[3] Such licenses, for example, grant permission to photocopy some music by certain artists and publishers for specific uses. Similarly, motion picture blanket licenses may be purchased, which allow for showing feature-length commercial videos that have been produced and distributed by a number of specified companies for use under certain conditions. These licenses apply to all of the settings of a church, including worship, social, and educational contexts. It is a good idea to purchase as many licenses as you can to compensate those whose materials you use, to protect yourself under the law, and to honor the intention of the law. When purchasing a blanket license, make sure that you know what each license covers and does not cover. The agreements will specify the companies, publishers, and artists whose works are covered. You may occasionally need to buy individual licenses to cover permission for use of individual films and songs. Costs will vary. The time it takes to receive permission varies, and the process may take as long as several months or as short as the time it takes to make one phone call. Generally, you will be able to find contact information listed on the material you wish to use. Company Web sites are often a good source for telephone numbers and details about license agreements. The blanket licenses mentioned above will help save a lot of time and resources.

I recommend buying the blanket licenses you will need to show movies and to reproduce and display hymns and songs. I also suggest that churches using multimedia become aware of certain provisions of copyright laws that directly apply to how churches may use copyrighted material in worship. What follows is intended to serve as information and not legal advice.

Do consult a lawyer if you have specific questions pertaining to copyright law and your use of worship multimedia.

The Worship Exemption

Copyright law protects original works of authorship and grants exclusive rights to copyright holders to do such things as reproduce, distribute, perform, and display the work.[4] The law provides some limitations to these rights under special circumstances. U.S. Code Section 110 lists specific limitations to the exclusive rights of copyright holders, and exempts certain performances and displays.

Section 110(3) of the code applies directly to the use of worship multimedia. Under this section of the law, churches are granted an "exemption of certain performances and displays . . . in the course of services at a place of worship. . . ." This includes "performance of a nondramatic literary or musical work or of a dramatico-musical work of a religious nature, or display of a work in the course of services at a place of worship or other religious assembly. . . ." This worship exemption is a "narrow exemption"[5] and must be carefully applied. While it allows for the use of certain material during worship, the provision does not apply to any other aspect of church life, such as educational and social occasions.

The Fair Use Doctrine

The fair use doctrine in Section 107 of the copyright law, like the worship exemption mentioned above, provides another limitation to exclusive rights. Fair use provides that "reproduction in copies or phonorecords . . . for purposes such as criticism, comment, news reporting, teaching (including multiple copies for classroom use), scholarship, or research, is not an infringement of copyright."

Fair use is determined by four factors:

1. the purpose and character of the use, including whether such use is of a commercial nature or is for nonprofit educational purposes
2. the nature of the copyrighted work
3. the amount and substantiality of the portion used in relation to the copyrighted work as a whole
4. the effect of the use upon the potential market for or value of the copyrighted work

While what constitutes fair use is the domain of the courts, a number of groups with direct interest in copyright law have agreed to specific voluntary standards for using multimedia in educational settings. While these guidelines do not specifically interpret the worship exemption of Section 110(3), they offer helpful interpretations of what constitutes fair use.

Fair Use Guidelines for Educational Multimedia

In 1996, the Subcommittee on Courts and Intellectual Property, Committee on the Judiciary, U.S. House of Representatives, consulted with hundreds of publishers, software companies, professional associations, organizations, libraries, governmental agencies, and educational institutions. This consortium of interested parties agreed upon certain "Fair Use Guidelines for Educational Multimedia" whose purpose was to "provide more specific guidelines that educators could follow and be reasonably sure that they would not be in violation of the copyright law."[6] The report offers "guidance on the application of the fair use exemption by educators, scholars and students in creating multimedia projects that include portions of copyrighted works, for their use in noncommercial educational activities, without having to seek the permission of copyright owners."[7] A final report was issued in 1998. While the guidelines are not legally binding, they "represent an agreed upon interpretation of the fair use provisions of the Copyright Act by the overwhelming majority of institutions and organizations affected by educational multimedia." I want to make clear that the "Fair Use Guidelines for Educational Multimedia" do not specifically apply to churches, yet they can provide churches with guidance for their use of multimedia in worship. Showing good faith, demonstrating awareness of the intricacies of copyright law, and understanding the unique application to educational and worship settings is advised.

The guidelines specify the portion of a work that may be included in a multimedia project. For example, they provide for using:

- Up to 10 percent or three minutes of motion media, meaning that clips from motion pictures should be three minutes or less in length.
- Up to 10 percent or 1,000 words of text.
- Ten percent but not more than 30 seconds of music, lyrics, and music video (however, ASCAP [American Society of Composers, Authors and Publishers] and BMI [an organization similar to ASCAP] say that

churches may play entire songs "as part of a worship service"). On its Web site, ASCAP advises churches that "Permission is not required for music played or sung as part of a worship service unless that service is transmitted beyond where it takes place (for example, a radio or television broadcast)."[8] BMI has confirmed the same in private correspondence.[9]

- Five photographic/illustration images by an artist or photographer, and not more than 10 percent or 15 images from a published collective work.

The guidelines provide limitations and reminders:

- No more than two usable copies may be kept or distributed.
- Multimedia projects may be kept for up to two years after its first instructional use, and beyond that time, permission of copyrighted portions of material is required.
- Sources must be credited with a display of copyright information, and this can be done in a separate section of the project except in certain circumstances where it is noticed on the image. Some advise having a slide at the beginning of the program indicating under what copyright guidelines copyrighted materials are used.
- Caution must be exercised in downloading material from the Internet. "Access to works on the Internet does not automatically mean that these can be reproduced and reused without permission or royalty payment and, furthermore, some copyrighted works may have been posted to the Internet without authorization of the copyright holder."[10]

By following these guidelines, worship leaders can be assured that they are working under standards developed and agreed to by a large number of parties with interest in applying copyright law to the use of multimedia. To summarize:

1. U.S. copyright law governs all use of copyrighted material. Churches must comply with the law.
2. The law allows "certain performances and displays . . . in the course of services at a place of worship" but other church settings (social and educational) not covered by this exemption may require additional permissions, licenses, or both.

3. "Fair Use Guidelines for Educational Multimedia" provide voluntary guidelines for the amount of such material that may be used, the length of time material may be stored before specific permissions are required, and for the proper crediting of sources of material.

Many Web sites offer the full text of Title 17, the Copyright Act of 1976, along with helpful discussions about various details of the law and how they may be applied. All churches and their leaders should be aware of how their church measures up to the law's requirements.

Fun with Equipment

So far, this chapter has primarily addressed the process of planning and creating multimedia worship. Multimedia worship leaders also need to think about how best to produce and deliver worship material to worshipers. For some people, these technical equipment aspects of multimedia worship are the fun part; however, not everyone enjoys dealing with equipment. While the whole matter may seem quite intimidating, it need not be. Bringing multimedia experiences into worship can be as easy as using a screen and a slide projector to project visual imagery while playing a CD through your existing sound system. To show a film clip, all you need is a television hooked up to a videocassette machine with a microphone placed at the TV speaker to amplify the sound.

Today's lightweight video-data projectors provide great versatility, as you can project movies from a videocassette recorder or DVD machine, and can display anything you see on a computer screen. Slides, pictures, and movies can all be run through a computer. It is possible to integrate video and audio through the computer so that all you need is a small projector and a laptop computer to present an entire audiovisual program. Many projectors may be used from either the front of a screen or from behind the screen. Rear-screen projection makes it possible to conceal the projector as well as the people running the equipment. Remote wireless technology allows a presenter to provide an entire program with a handheld control.

Multimedia technology changes rapidly, and this means that equipment is outdated rather quickly. What we have found, however, is that older equipment having adequate processing speed, memory, and data storage capacity may work just fine. Our projector, for example, has lasted four years without needing a bulb change. We have gone through three generations of computers, however, just to provide better image quality and to be able to show movies that are embedded into the software. You may discover that while prices of equipment have stabilized, you get faster processors and more capabilities with each new technical development. Our worship team recommends this list of minimal equipment needed to produce and present multimedia worship.[11]

• An LCD projector with a minimum bulb brightness of 750 lumens is recommended, depending on your light conditions in a worship space. Projectors with 1,000 lumens or more are commonly available and reasonably priced. A video projector projects computer and video images from 3 to 16 feet at 40 to 200 inches diagonal. The advantage of these machines over TV monitors is they provide a larger image and greater portability, since they are often the size of a small suitcase. The advantage of a portable projector is it can be occasionally used in other parts of the church facility. The projector uses a single lens, much like a slide projector. While the expense of such equipment increases with lumen output of the projection lamps, more lumens provide a much brighter image. The cost of video projectors has come down considerably in recent years.

• A surround-sound stereo is really nice, but not necessary. You will want to be able to input a number of sources including compact discs (CDs), computer, videotape (VHS) and videodisc (DVD) movies. Our church has used three levels of sound systems. The first was a TV with a microphone held to the speaker so people could hear it through the existing sound system. We brought in a portable CD player to play music. The second generation was installing a home entertainment surround-sound system to which we hooked a CD player, videocassette player, and a computer. Our latest system is a new soundboard and speakers through which all of our equipment is mixed.

• We started out with a single videocassette player and then upgraded to a dual-deck player so we could have two clips cued at one time.
• A DVD player makes it easy to cue movies and begin them more precisely than with videotape. There can be a frustrating time delay with DVD, however, as one must wait an average of 50 seconds for the disk to cycle to the main menu before being able to search for the scene.

- We have recently discovered that a video-capture board, an internal card that may be installed in a computer, or an external device connected through a computer's USB port, can provide for copying short sequences from either videotape or DVD. This material can then be saved as a file that can be exported directly into Microsoft PowerPoint or other software and then displayed. Because of this feature, we seldom use actual videotape or DVD in worship, as the short-film segments are viewed by simply clicking a slide in the PowerPoint program.

- Multiple-disc CD player, allowing for several CDs to be ready to play.

- Printer to print out handouts of worship slides and order of worship for worship leaders.

- Computer with:
  - Minimum 512 MB RAM (better: 1 GB RAM)
  - 40 GB Hard Drive
  - Rewriteable CD drive (for transporting or storing materials between computers)
  - 17-inch monitor

- Microsoft Office 2000 professional software. There are many computer software products that make presenting pictures, words, and video easy with the computer and projector. Before deciding upon which software your church should use, consider who will be using it. There is software that is widely available and easy to learn, and there are more complex programs with added features, and a longer learning curve. Our media team recommends this: call your school district and find out what presentation software your children and youth are using. If you want them to become an important part of your multimedia worship, get the software that they are using. The children and youth of your church will bring the next generation along. Worship truly becomes the work of the people . . . all the people, no matter their age.

Equipment and other resources helpful to have:

- small TV for cueing movie clips
- digital camera
- mixing board for controlling sound outputs

Figure 3

This shows the kinds of equipment that may be used to produce and present multimedia worship. This equipment is on a cart in a chancel and situated behind the projection screen. Included are A) screen B) rear-screen LCD projector C) computer monitor D) computer keyboard E) printer F) small monitor to view video G) DVD player H) 5-disc CD changer I) dual-cassette VHS machine J) cassette audio tape player K) sound amplifiers L) resource shelf M) computer tower N) sound board O) sound monitor.

- laptop computer for portability
- additional and portable sound system for use beyond the sanctuary
- additional monitor for choir or other areas that cannot see the screen
- Internet access

We also added another computer at church so that those without home computers can come to church and work on song and video productions. Buying this computer meant we could use the computer in the worship area mainly for presentation rather than for production. Our team prefers to have fewer people using the main sanctuary computer to minimize technical glitches, and encourages more people using the second computer in another part of the building.

As noted above, presentation technology, like all technologies, is advancing at a rapid pace. Churches using multimedia will want to pay attention to recent developments in technology. Although churches probably do not want to update their equipment with every technology improvement—it probably is not good stewardship of resources to do so—there are ways they can be kept reasonably up-to-date without incurring great expense. As companies and schools move into advanced technology, they trade in their older equipment. Churches can find refurbished equipment at very reasonable prices, with costs in the hundreds rather than the thousands of dollars. Many church members are upgrading their own computer equipment on an annual basis and have older equipment ready to donate. Such equipment is always a starting point for churches wanting to experiment with what the technology can offer to enhance education and worship. Once your congregation sees and hears how this equipment helps you provide memorable and powerful worship services, they will find ways to finance better and newer equipment.

There are many resource people, companies, and books that can help churches determine the appropriate, affordable equipment they will need to produce multimedia worship. Many school systems, public libraries, and businesses are using integrated presentation technologies as tools to accomplish their mission. Church people may consider consulting with college and university teachers, business leaders, school-district librarians and multimedia specialists, as well as public librarians to learn about their experience with multimedia equipment. Sales representatives of companies specializing in providing churches with projectors, computers, screens, and sound equipment may be invited in for consultations. Many congregations are discovering that their own members have access to multimedia equipment, and can borrow it from their place of work or institution for a weekend's trial. Fortunately, you are not on your own with these matters, and you can learn from many sources.

Screens

One of the most important equipment decisions has to do with projection screens. The screen can be a vehicle for God's revelatory power, opening imaginations in fresh new ways, attracting attention, fostering understanding, and stimulating mission response. Installing them in our sanctuaries requires some forethought and planning.

What kind of a screen should you use? Some of the variables that must be considered include the size of the worship group, the nature of the worship space, and the financial resources that you have. Twenty-seven-inch TV screens with sound amplified through the sound system of the sanctuary (with the aid of a microphone) would be suitable for many settings. Additional TV screens may be used for people seated in the back, or in choir areas. Large-screen TVs are becoming less costly, but the larger the TV, the heavier it is and the less mobile it will be. A lighter-weight, more mobile option is to use a large screen and a video projector that allows you to adjust the image size to fill the screen. NEC Technologies suggests that generally, for 50 persons, you would use a 72-inch screen measured diagonally. For groups of around 150, use a 120-inch screen; 225 people, 150-inch screen; 400 people, 200-inch screen; and 900 people, 300-inch screen.[12] Screens may stand on tripods, be attached to walls and pulled down manually, or may be electrically controlled and retractable at the push of a button. The old filmstrip-projector or slide-projector screens will work fine, but the video image may not be as clear as that provided with special video screens. The same is true for a light-colored wall. Video screens range in cost from hundreds to thousands of dollars, depending on size and whether they come on a simple frame or require electrical up and down motors and switches.

Deciding where to put a screen in a sanctuary that has not been built for one can be difficult. You want to begin by looking at the space and what is already there. Decisions about where to place the screen are best made in relationship to the architectural design of the sanctuary. The architect

Figure 4

This shows two screens mounted on walls above the speaking platform. Ceiling mounted projectors may be used to project images on the screens. Some churches install projection rooms behind these screens and then conceal rear-image projectors in them. These are permanent screens that may be concealed with cloth.

who planned your sanctuary did so knowing it was to be a place of worship. How does what you see contribute to setting a visual tone for worship? How does what you see function in the life of the worshiping congregation? One way to discover this for yourself is to sit in your sanctuary and look at the architectural details. What sort of ceiling does the sanctuary have? Follow the lines of beam and ceiling and notice how your eye moves across these features. Where is the choir positioned in the sanctuary? How much glass is there and how does it contribute to the sacred space? What does the amount of light coming into your sanctuary, naturally and artificially, tell you about the meaning of light in your church? Will you have to reduce that light in order to see images on a screen? Where is the communion table or altar located? Is there a baptismal font? What is the meaning of its location? What religious symbolism do you see in such things as the number of hanging lights, the placement of the cross, the arrangement of organ pipes, the positioning of lectern and pulpit? Where is the Bible located? Do you have flags or other banners standing or hanging in the sanctuary? Are there candles?

Notice every visual detail you see and think about what these elements are saying about your worship life. Do the details lead you to think about God? In what ways? What features are prominent and which are subtler? Is the cross emphasized or de-emphasized? What elements contribute to the feeling of sacred space? Your observations will help you understand where to position your screen. Is it possible to find a location where the screen neither interrupts the architectural lines nor obscures an important detail in the sanctuary?

Next, find one of the screens your church has used and put it in various spots in your sanctuary. What does it look like in those various positions? What does it conceal? What does it reveal? Where would you place your projection equipment? What would this equipment conceal or reveal? Consulting with projection or screen sales personnel, church architects, and your own committees will help your church arrive at the best solutions to your technical and architectural concerns.

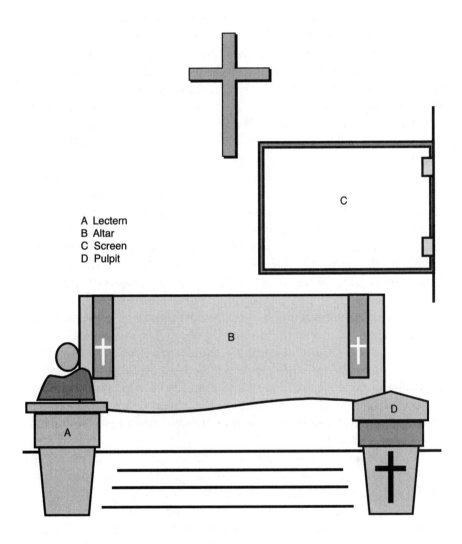

A Lectern
B Altar
C Screen
D Pulpit

Figure 5

Some screens are permanently installed, yet visible only as needed.
In this case, a lightweight screen is attached to a wall with two hinges.
It is pulled outward when in use, and rests against the wall at other times.
Motorized retractable screens may come up from the floor or scroll
down from a ceiling or wall.

Frequently Asked Questions

The following questions are grouped into three areas: technical, organizational, and artistic.

Technical Questions

Should we use videocassettes, DVD, or both?

DVD works nicely because it allows you to locate scenes very easily. Movie scenes are organized in numbered units, and as with a book, are called "chapters." The content of the chapters is listed on the DVD cover or inside it on a separate sheet. These chapters will also include where they are in relationship to the time elapsed in the film (in hours, minutes, and seconds). To locate a scene, all you do is skip to the chapter where you know it is located, and play it, keeping track of the chapter number, the hour, minute, and second where the scene begins, and where it ends. This allows you to easily cue the scene for replay, and to end it exactly at the point you want it stopped. A downside of DVD is that you have to wait an average time of around 50 seconds as the DVD cycles to the main menu before you can access your scene. Showing multiple DVD scenes becomes difficult because of the menu delay, and then having to search for the chapter and time sequence. This is still easier and faster than cueing videotape, which is also cued by noting the hour, minute, and second where you want to begin your scene, and end it. Some video machines do not have as clean of a start and stop as DVD players. Having a two-deck VCR is helpful, however, when you want to have scenes from two different movies ready to go.

We have found a better technology with a video capture board that is either installed into a computer, or purchased as an external device that can be plugged into the computer. This hardware, along with the accompanying software, allows you to copy short scenes in DVD and VHS formats, edit them, and insert them into your presentation software (such as PowerPoint). Having DVD, VHS, and video capture capabilities increases your production and presentation options, and the more choices you have, the better off you are.

Which presentation software should we use?

There are so many products out there, and every one has a "learning curve" of a dozen hours or more. Something to consider when deciding upon particular software is what the members of the congregation are already using. What presentation software are the teenagers learning in school? What do most of your congregation's members use at home? Since you will want these people to be doing much of the creative work of producing multimedia programs and showing them during worship, it makes sense to use software that they already are using.

How much video should we use in a service?

If you are voluntarily using the "Fair Use Guidelines for Educational Multimedia,"[1] you may show three minutes or less of any one video. Even if you plan to use more of a movie because you have a license to do so, our experience is that short film clips make their point very well. What you want is interaction between your media and your message, not people just sitting and watching a lot of video. We have found that using three or four short video sequences in a 35-minute worship service provide a nice balance between the spoken message and the multimedia message.

May we copy a show from television (like CNN or a soap opera) and use a section of it in worship?

A congressional committee produced "Guidelines for Off-air Recording of Broadcast Programming for Educational Purposes" in 1981 to provide guidance for teachers in school settings.[2] The rules were written to apply to the three main commercial networks and to public broadcasting, and separate rules have been drawn up for cable, satellite, and distance learning settings. The 1981 rules provided that taped shows could not be kept for more than 45 days after the recording date, must be shown in the first 10 days of that period, may be shown only twice, and must include the copyright notice as recorded on the broadcast program. While these rules were not written for churches, they do provide a rule of thumb by which you might try to use such material in the worship setting only, consistent with the choice to follow the "Fair Use Guidelines for Educational Multimedia."

Our sanctuary is full of natural light and there is no way we can get a projector and screen with a bright-enough image. Now what do we do?

There are projectors that are bright enough to show imagery in well-lit conditions, but the cost of such equipment might be more than your church can afford. If budget is a concern, and your worship space is just too bright, consider going to an evening service when daylight is not a factor.

We have a screen that is just used to show words. How do we start adding pictures?

Get a digital camera and photograph church members in action. Be sure the photos do not look staged—try to minimize your shots of folks standing in rows smiling at the camera, and make sure you can clearly see the subjects' faces. Take pictures of the youth group at play, or the seniors at lunch, or the church school children in a learning situation. Take the youth group to the nursing home to visit church members, and bring the camera along. Show pictures like these before the worship service begins. Demonstrate the power of visuals. Start simply, and use imagery sparingly and purposefully.

What do you do when the computer freezes, or some other equipment does not work, and you are in the middle of the worship service?

What I do is explain that there is an obvious technical difficulty, and give 20 to 30 seconds for the team to address it. If they need more time, I tell a little story about technology glitches I have experienced before, at grocery stores, airports, and so forth. A little humor defuses any tension. If it seems that what you wanted to show will not be coming on for a while, you can explain what it was you were going to see, and move on with your presentation without the visuals. Remember to say something like you are not a television network, just amateurs trying to do your best for the sake of the church. The presenter should be pretty good at ad-libbing!

Organizational FAQ's

How do you find people to serve on teams?

I like how Bill Easum puts it: when you talk about what you want to do, see whose eyes light up. Tell people, committees, and groups about the skills you are seeking. Ask around the church, and the larger community, to find out names of people who know how to do what you want to do. Invite them into your planning sessions. Since multimedia requires a variety of talents and skills, spread your net widely and see what you bring in.

I am in a little church with a small average worship attendance. They will never go for multimedia, but I still think it is a good idea. What do I do?

Be clear about your vision with the church leadership. Remind them that what you are trying to do is effectively serve the congregation's mission and ministry. A powerful way to do that is to add visuals to worship to help tell the story about your church's history and purpose, mission and vision. Try introducing some of the steps we talked about in chapter 2. Explain along the way that some of your church's inactive members may be looking for another door into the church, and that door might just be a multimedia worship service. This door may also attract people in the community who might be willing to come and share their area of technical and productive expertise. Inviting these people to join in a new service planning process may begin to build the congregation in new ways. Multimedia worship is another way to involve the youth and children of the congregation. Few people argue with children and youth ministries.

With different volunteers producing media art for worship, how do we maintain theological consistency in what we offer?

It is important to hold regular and frequent group discussions about what you are doing, and why. Read scripture and learn to talk about your theological viewpoints together. People will value this regular discussion about scripture, faith, life, and their church's mission. They will become more aware of one another's theological similarities and differences, and through discussion that respects different views, will grow a consensus for planning, developing, and leading worship. Hold regular discussions about the messages you are intending to communicate and talk about the media, imagery, and illustrations that best communicate the message, and why. You may want to have a lead theologian or executive producer who understands your congregation's theological framework. This may be the pastor or a lay leader. It is this person's responsibility to assure that words, imagery, and music comply with the production guidelines you have set for yourselves. Your regular team and occasional producers of material will need to understand that sometimes the executive producer may need to make slight adjustments like changing an image, removing a video sequence, or adapting words in order to follow your guidelines.

How do you provide ongoing training for your teams?

You can provide quick training or 10- to 15-minute sessions at weekly team meetings where you reflect on what went well and what did not at your previous worship service, and why. Take some time to practice your craft with each other, sharing computer hints, talking about important scenes in recent movies, or discussing how a current song heard on the radio might help illustrate a coming scriptural theme. You could schedule longer training sessions at quarterly gatherings or schedule an annual retreat. Make it clear to one another that you are always teaching and learning together. Review some of your past work, or something someone is now working on, and talk about how these things might be done differently, why certain imagery was selected, or how the music and imagery fit the theme it was supporting. Doing this requires that trust develop among the team. Leaders will want to try to build trust in the group and model good communication skills. Team leaders might want to model ways to ask questions, listen, and speak as a way to develop a style of team communication.

How do we prevent our volunteers from burning out?

These strategies will all help to keep new energy coming into the core team, and help maintain their creativity.

- Keep talking honestly with each other about time commitments and expectations.
- Talk together about the intrinsic rewards and personal satisfaction that come from being involved in satisfying ministry.
- Give volunteers educational opportunities. Learn together. Keep working at improving media skills such as putting pictures to music.
- Provide for recognition of volunteers' work before the whole church. Keep in mind that different people value different types of recognition. Some people do not feel thanked unless it happens in public; some think public thanks are cheap and easy and much prefer a note, letter, or heartfelt, face-to-face thank-you.
- Continue to recruit new people and ask them to attend occasional planning sessions. Encourage the entire church to suggest film clips and music to your team. This helps assure a source of fresh material, and helps expand the musical styles and film choices that may be used. Our team has found that personal, face-to-face invitations work the best for encouraging new people to share their ideas and to come to occasional meetings. Getting new people involved, even if on a minimal basis, helps reduce the weekly planning and production pressure a team will sometimes feel.
- Give volunteers time off.
- Regularly celebrate the contributions of your team with social gatherings and fun times together.

Is multimedia worship really worth the time and effort?

Producing and providing multimedia worship services can uncover some of the hidden talents in a congregation. The entire process of providing multimedia worship experiences can result in many levels of growth: spiritual, relationship, learning, worship attendance, mission awareness, and membership. New energy flows into a congregation as the people who grow to support this with their money, their time, and their talents.

I am used to being in sole control of planning and presenting worship, so how do I let go of control and develop a team approach to planning and presenting worship?

Get in touch with your leadership style and your comfort or discomfort levels with control, and being out of control. Learn to listen to your team members. Help train them in theology and presentation skills so they become comfortable expressing their gifts, and you become comfortable allowing new styles and approaches into worship. Given the chance, they will help train you to learn to become a better team member.

How do worship leaders find time and energy to add another worship service to the schedule?

Adding another service or increasing the use of multimedia in worship may require adjusting work priorities so that the focus becomes worship leadership, planning, and presentation. What are you doing now that another member of the body of Christ could be doing, and even better than you? How much time do you spend on tasks that do not relate to the central mission of your church? Can you identify a small group in the church who may be interested in working with you to add another service? Trying this for 12 weeks, and then evaluating before continuing, is a way to learn together by your own experience. Worship leaders must also be willing to share responsibility with teams. A leader engaging in self-care practices will help maintain creative energy and sustain the transition into different ways of leading worship.

We have people who will not come to church if we start using media and technology. What do we do then?

No matter what we try, someone will stay away for some reason. They may, after a while, come to see the benefits of the media. I think it is a good idea to gradually introduce multimedia worship, and to have a separate service for a more intensive use of media, rather than requiring that everyone adjust to it. There may be some members who believe the church should not use screen technologies at all. You might not be able to reason with one or two of them, and you must weigh their objection against all the positive results flowing from what you are doing.

Our pastor is totally against using pictures in worship, but some of us want to use them. What do we do?

Try to negotiate an agreement to use the pictures before worship begins, perhaps in the announcement time. Another option might be to use them in a different setting of the church. It is possible that after seeing the benefits of adding visual experiences in other areas of the life of the church, the pastor and congregation may come to agree to occasional uses in worship.

What surprises can I expect?

Your church may change! If you start a separate multimedia service, you may discover that it draws more attendance than another service. You might have to think about what to do with your traditional service if it begins to decline. Then you will have to address issues of whether you will add to the budget to support an ongoing multimedia service, staff it, buy more equipment, and so forth.

Another surprise is that some extremely committed people will begin to take ownership of the multimedia service and become protective of it, supportive of it, and evangelical about it. This is a good thing, and leaders will want to affirm this support while continuing to grow the whole church, not just the media service or the media people.

Artistic FAQs

Is there ever a moment when there is just too much on the screen?

There can be a point of sensory overload and the use of too many visuals. Occasionally, you might want to use a blank screen, ask people to close their eyes, spend some time in silence, or otherwise block out external stimulation. Remember that the media serve your message, rather than the message serving the media.

What happens if the pictures someone selected to illustrate a song does not match with what a piece of music is about, or match with our theme?

A small adjustment can make a big difference in communicating a theme. I spoke in another chapter about how we removed a picture of the White House that was being associated with the lyric, "Would you teach your children to tell the truth?" because we felt the picture would distract people from understanding the main message we were communicating through the song. By changing one picture out of 35 slides, we were able to assure a consistency of music, message, and that day's worship theme. Our team has found that if there is any doubt about how a song or its accompanying pictures fit the worship theme, that by simply adding a slide of the worship scripture text, they can keep the song's relationship to our theme clear.

What are inappropriate uses of media in worship?

Video or music is inappropriate when the segments are too long, do not clearly relate to the theme of the worship service, or do not conform to your own guidelines and standards. Using anything that does not carefully follow copyright law is also inappropriate.

How can you be sure a song and its imagery really fit your theme?

Nailing your theme requires clear communication between a planning team and a person producing a particular piece of media. It is helpful to explain—in a sentence or two, not a paragraph—to a volunteer the direction of a service and how a piece of media fits into that service. If you cannot explain the theme and how the pieces connect in just a few sentences, worshipers themselves will probably not make the connections. Make suggestions about the types of pictures that would fit the song and the theme. Our producers report that they like knowing the service theme and a suggested direction for the media they are producing.

Is it appropriate to play country music in church?

I answer this question with more questions. The larger question here is, What music fits the worship guidelines you have developed? Will you allow music from popular culture, like country, rock, folk, or rap, or only from music from high culture, like classical and some jazz? What kind of music helps us worship God, and why? How does a particular piece of music help us experience God, worship God, learn about God, and thank God? How does a piece of music help us understand our relationship with God, others, and ourselves? What song lyrics help us do this? Are you able to make a clear connection between a piece of music and some aspect of your worship theme and direction? Once you answer these questions, you should be able to answer whether you will allow country music, or any other kind of popular music to serve God in worship. Remember to pay attention to what church members are listening to, and that what is appropriate in one congregation might not work in another.

Is there such a thing as using too much media in worship?

Yes. Using too much media can call attention to itself rather than to the larger worship purpose. Using too much media can overload people and they may start tuning it out. People may be too stimulated, may miss the point of the media, or lose interest. There is no guarantee that just because you use movies or popular music they will fit a service. A good interactive service must find a balance between the use of media, the oral contributions of the worship leader, and the participation of the congregation. An interactive worship means that everyone involved will be interacting with the message at some level, rather than thinking about other things.

What do you do if the wrong movie scene is shown on screen, or the wrong words come out?

Once I asked our technical team to stop the DVD in the middle of a film clip when I realized they had played the wrong scene. Having seen the film myself, I knew that had it continued, we would have seen something we really should not in worship. Luckily we stopped it in time. Another time, as I have explained, a profanity slipped out, and we had to address it and be up front about the mistake. Better technology and good preparation helps minimize if not eliminate most of these problems. Better technology provides a way to delete a word or scene. Better preparation means the production team knows when to turn the sound down on a song if there is a lyric we do not want to include.

How do you decide which themes you will use to serve as the focus for a service?

This usually results from a collaborative effort between many different groups with interest in worship planning. Those responsible for planning and leading worship will want to get suggestions for coming services from sources like the Christian education committee (who will be planning weekly church school lessons that could be used for worship themes), the media team, the congregation itself, and the clergy (who might want to follow the rhythms of the church year and look at the lessons in the lectionary, which grows out of those rhythms).

What if our worship team cannot think of any media to use to illustrate a theme?

Start brainstorming well in advance so you can have a working list of songs and recent films. Since you would know the general worship themes as long as a year in advance and the specific worship themes for a month or two in advance, you could search out lectionary or sermon resources for ideas. Web sites like www.textweek.com provide a list of lectionary passages, worship themes, and suggestions for films and art that fit.

What criteria do you use to decide how much or what part of a movie to use?

As you view movie scenes with the team, keep talking about the worship theme and the scriptural focus. Watch for how closely the scenes come to illustrating the theme and focus. While it is often obvious when a scene works or not, what may seem obvious to one member of the team may not appear so to another person. Talk together about how a scene does or does not help interpret the worship message that you are presenting. When a scene seems to have a loose connection to the message, but is still deemed important enough to include, practice explaining the connection to one another. This will help when you explain it to the worship congregation. Try to explain the connection in only one or two sentences.

Is it OK to use a song or film clip more than once?

Showing material you have used before seems to be acceptable on an occasional basis. We have reused some songs three to four times, but simply changed pictures to help the song illustrate a different theme or approach. We have used a particular video scene two to three times because the message was important enough to repeat. While people may remember that you have used something before, this will likely be acceptable, as they understand the media is illustrating something new.

A Service of Dedication for a Sanctuary Projection Screen

I have seen services of dedication for all kinds of different equipment and furnishings used in and around churches, so why not one for a projection screen? This brief dedication is designed for inclusion in a service of worship.

If you are already equipped to project words and images on a screen, you could display the words for this service. Be sure to include images along with the words. Your opening slide could be a picture of the screen in the sanctuary. Why the screen itself? It is a surprising image, so it will capture attention, and it represents the object you are dedicating. The screen will be used to represent a number of visuals. Seeing the image of the screen on the screen is a subtle reminder that what you see on the screen is only a representation of reality, not reality itself. Another image you might consider projecting is a photograph of your worshiping congregation. Across the picture put the words, "A Service of Dedication for a Sanctuary Projection Screen."

As appropriate, position yourself and any committee members near the screen so you are able to gesture towards it and touch it. You do this as a visual reminder to the congregation that the screen is something that is used by church leaders to serve the church's purposes. The screen has no authority of its own.

A Service of Dedication

LEADER: Our church has purchased this screen [*gesture towards the screen*], along with the equipment [*gesture towards it*] that is generating the images and words that we see. These have been purchased with gifts from (memorial gift, special gift, donations, bequest, etc.) that *has/have* been generously given to the glory of God. Let us join together now in our litany of dedication.

LEADER: We gather here to worship and praise God, creator of heaven and earth, who by the power of word said, "Let there be light."

CONGREGATION: **We thank God for creative power revealed to us in word and light.**

LEADER: By the light of a burning bush, Moses heard the word of God and was sent to free the slaves and lead them towards a land of freedom.

CONGREGATION: **We thank God for saving power revealed to us in word and light.**

LEADER: God's light and voice were present at the Transfiguration of Jesus.

CONGREGATION: **We thank God for Jesus, the word of life and the light of truth.**

LEADER: We celebrate God's promise that at the end of time there will be a New Jerusalem, a city that "has no need of sun or moon to shine on it, for the glory of God is its light" (Rev. 21:23).

CONGREGATION: **We worship the God of word and light.**

LEADER: Eternal God, we thank you for your inspiring, creative presence made known through your Holy Spirit, and we ask your blessing on the creative efforts of this church to learn of you, to worship you, and to love you.

We remember that you told Noah how to build your ark of salvation. Over time you have brought us new technologies, that your love and salvation may extend to all the ends of the earth.

Build within us humble and faithful hearts. May what is shown on this screen lead us to greater service in your world. Help us to honor Jesus, who told us to "let your light shine before others, so that they may see your good works and give glory" to you (Matt. 5:16).

Bless those who will interpret your scripture through words and imagery in this sanctuary. Remind us that you have set before us a path for life, to do justice, to love mercy, and to walk humbly with you.

CONGREGATION: **Amen.**

Hymn of Dedication[1]

> For the joy of ear and eye,
> For the heart and mind's delight,
> For the mystic harmony
> Linking sense with sound and sight,
> · Lord of all to thee we raise
> This our hymn of grateful praise.

Words of Dedication

Leader and Congregation: We, the members of this church, dedicate this screen to God's glory, that it may help us know God's light, better understand God's word, and respond to God's call to go into the world as servants of joy, love, and peace.

1 Multimedia and Worship

1. The periodical was the *Congregationalist and Christian World* and the article was "The Case for Motion Pictures, Part I" by George J. Anderson. It is quoted from Terry Lindvall, *The Silents of God: Selected Issues and Documents in Silent American Film and Religion 1908–1925* (Lanham, Md.: Scarecrow Press, Inc., 2001), 39–40.

2. Ibid., 188, 181.

3. Ibid., 73.

4. Robert Webber, "The Effects of Technology upon Worship," *Worship Leader* 10, no. 4 (2002): 12.

5. Sally Morgenthaler, "Worship in the Digital Age," *Worship Leader* 10, no. 4 (2002): 23.

6. Peter Robb, *Midnight in Sicily* (New York: Vintage Books, 1996), 89.

7. Susan White, *Christian Worship and Technological* Change (Nashville: Abingdon Press, 1994), 18.

8. Mitchell Stephens, *The Rise of the Image and the Fall of the Word* (New York: Oxford University Press, 1998), 33.

9. See White, p. 80, and her discussion about "The Biotechnology of Communion."

10. Sally McFague, *Life Abundant: Rethinking Theology and Economy for a Planet in Peril* (Minneapolis: Fortress Press, 2001), 13.

11. Ben Logan, ed. Television Awareness Training (New York: Media Action Research Center, 1977).

12. Gregoria and Jeanne-Marie Ferreras-Oleffe, "New Language, New Formation," *Lumen Vitae: The International Review of Religious Education* 33, No. 2 (1978): 238–239.

13. Mgr. Lucien M. Metzinger, "Audiovisuals and Evangelicization," *Lumen Vitae: The International Review of Religious Education* 33, No. 2 (1978): 145.

14. See Barry Sanders, *A is for Ox: The Collapse of Literacy and the Rise of Violence in an Electronic Age* (New York: Vintage Books, 1994), 111. Sanders tells of how a mother bear must lick the stomach of her newborn cub for it to mature.

15. Brad Hansen, *The Dictionary of Multimedia* (Wilson, Ore.: Franklin, Beedle & Associates, 1997), v–vi.

16. Ibid.

17. Ibid.

18. Jim Collins, *Good to Great: Why Some Companies Make the Leap . . . and Others Don't* (New York: HarperBusiness, 2001).

19. Jim Collins, "How Great Companies Tame Technology," *Newsweek*, April 29, 2002, 51.

20. Walter Brueggemann, *Texts Under Negotiation* (Minneapolis: Fortress Press, 1993), 24.

21. Ibid., 24–25.

22. Ibid., 24.

23. Mark Chaves, *How Do We Worship?* (Bethesda, Md.: The Alban Institute, 1999), 6.

24. From literature distributed by Fowler, Inc., a multimedia equipment company specializing in serving churches.

25. I thank the pastors involved in the online course I taught through the University of Dubuque Theological Seminary's Certificate in Technology and Ministry program (August–December 2001) for sharing with me how their churches have used multimedia in worship. Eileen Crowley-Horak refers to the Ohio congregation in her doctoral work (see n. 28 below) and *United Church News*, a national publication of the United Church of Christ, featured the Arizona congregation in its June 2001 issue.

26. These comments describe some of the things the pastors in my online course learned through their worship and media experiments in their own congregations. I am grateful to the following for their reflections: Frank Boerema, Sam Massey, Sarah Johnsen, Wes Pixler, Bill Taylor, and Wade Kirsteatter.

27. I thank Sarah Johnsen, Eric Elnes, Bill Rishel, and Jim Martin for these statements. The Elnes comment is from Cliff Aerie, "Arizona church melds arts, technology" in *United Church News*, June 2001.

28. Quotations are from members of the Union-Congregational UCC of Waupun, Wisconsin: Neil Gleason, Sheryl Searvogel, Ross Dary, Jeff Duchac, and Lisa Lenz. They were given during the field research of Eileen Crowley-Horak for "Testing the Fruits: Liturgical Aesthetics as Applied to Liturgical Media Art," dissertation for the faculty of Union Theological Seminary, New York, 2002.

29. Webber, "The Effects of Technology upon Worship."

30. Marva Dawn, *Reaching Out without Dumbing Down* (Grand Rapids, Mich.: William B. Eerdmans Publishing Company, 1995), 292.

31. Chaves, *How Do We Worship?*, 7.

32. Eileen Crowley-Horak, "Theories of the Creative Audience and Implications for Development of a Theory of the Creative Worshiping Audience" (Unpublished paper, August 21, 2000, Union Theological Seminary, New York).

33. From "For the Beauty of the Earth" by Folliott S. Pierpoint as found in *The Pilgrim Hymnal* (New York: The Pilgrim Press, 1931, renewed 1986), no. 366.

2 Strategies for Developing Support

1. Lindvall, *The Silents of God*, 72.

2. Collins, *Good to Great*, 183.

3. I also used recommendations found in Jane Westberg and Jason Hilliard, *Teaching Creatively with Video: Fostering Reflection, Communication, and Other Skills* (New York: Springer Publishing Company, 1994), 14. Short clips or "video triggers" are used "for stimulating discussion (and) provoking intellectual and emotional reactions" and are best used by a presenter who makes introductory comments to "set the stage and present a challenge to their learners" (p. 55).

4. In an online e-mail seminar, a pastor asked Bill Easum how to start a process for growing a church. Easum wrote that he should get a vision, "then share it and watch whose eyes light up." This conversation took place as part of Easum's "transformational leadership" online forum on February 9, 1998.

5. Jim Collins confirms this approach: "After five years of research, I'm absolutely convinced that if we just focus our attention on the right things—and stop doing the senseless things that consume so much time

and energy—we can create a powerful Flywheel Effect without increasing the number of hours we work." This quotation is from his article, "Good to Great" in *Fast Company* magazine, October 2001, p. 104. You can find this and other articles about organizational change and leadership at www.fastcompany.com.

3 Learning to Use Film, Art, and Music

1. I thank the Rev. Kendell Nordstrom for this story.
2. Reported in "Fact Sheets on Media Use" by the National Institute on Media and the Family at www.mediaandthefamily.org.
3. Ibid.
4. Doug Adams, *Eyes to See Wholeness: Visual Arts Informing Biblical and Theological Studies in Education and Worship through the Church Year* (Prescott, Ariz.: Educational Ministries, Inc., 1995), 107.
5. Tex Sample, *The Spectacle of Worship in a Wired World: Electronic Culture and the Gathered People of God* (Nashville: Abingdon Press, 1998), 46.
6. Quoted in Eileen Crowley-Horak, "Aesthetics for Navigating the 'Twilight Zone' of Media Arts in Liturgy" (Unpublished paper, April 26, 2001, Union Theological Seminary, New York), 38.
7. From Eileen Crowley-Horak, "Testing the Fruits: Liturgical Aesthetics as Applied to Liturgical Media Art," Dissertation (Unpublished) (New York: Union Theological Seminary, 2002), 13.
8. Eileen Crowley-Horak, "Testing the Fruits," 6.
9. Sister Wendy Beckett, *A Child's Book of Prayer in Art* (New York: Dorling Kindersley Publishing, Inc. 1995), 6.
10. John Dillenberger, *A Theology of Artistic Sensibilities: The Visual Arts and the Church* (New York: Crossroad, 1969), 242.
11. For a discussion about the "form-content-meaning" process of studying art, see Erwin Panofsky, *Studies in Iconology: Humanistic Themes in the Art of the Renaissance* (New York: Oxford University Press, 1939), 3–17.
12. Most school districts, and some churches, have developed policies of "implied consent" where a person's permission to be photographed is assumed, and it is understood that such pictures and video may occasionally be used in publications and presentations. An "opt out" form is made available

for those who do not wish to have their pictures taken and used for such purposes. Contact your local school district for a sample of such a policy and form.

13. I thank the Rev. Jennifer Dawson for sharing this with me.

14. Michael Rhodes Films is producing "Film Clips," regularly distributed videotapes of short scenes used by the permission of major motion picture studios. The tape of clips is accompanied by a study guide for use in discussions and as worship illustrations. More information is available at www.filmclipsonline.com. Edward McNulty, who is working with Rhodes on this project, has been finding theological themes in films for over three decades. A list of films, theological themes, and other resources may be found at his website, www.visualparables.com, or by calling (800) 528-6522.

15. Wholly Mackeral Productions, *A Media Sourcebook* (Berkeley, Calif.: Pacific School of Religion, 1973). Warren Mullen and Julius Young developed the list of songs and themes for the music chapter. For a more recent discussion of popular music and faith connections, see Darrell Cluck, Catherine George, and Clinton McCann, *Facing the Music: Faith and Meaning in Popular Songs* (St. Louis: Chalice Press, 1999). McCann, evangelical professor of biblical interpretation at Eden Theological Seminary, teaches with songs and videos that contain what he calls biblical and theological "allusions, themes, directions, and/or ethical significance."

16. See B. Lee Cooper, "Teaching with Popular Music Resources: A Bibliography of Interdisciplinary Instructional Approaches" in *Popular Music and Society*, Summer 1998.

17. Leonard Sweet used the phrase "cultural circumcision" in his presentation at the Federated Church of Green Lake, Wisconsin, on March 3, 2002.

4 Producing Multimedia Worship

1. This conversation took place as part of Easum's "transformational leadership" online forum on February 9, 1998.

2. I am grateful to Teri Dary, a leading member of our multimedia worship team, for developing these standards for slides.

3. LicenSing provides a license to use copyright-cleared music for worship (Logos Productions, (800) 328-0200). Motion picture or video

licenses and music licenses are also available from CCLI (Christian Copyright Licensing International) at www.ccli.com or (800) 234-2446. A blanket video license is available through the Motion Picture Licensing Corporation, www.mplc.com or (800) 462-8855.

4.   Many Web sites offer the full text of Title 17, the Copyright Act of 1976, along with links to helpful discussions about various details of the law and how these may be applied. Two good sites are the U.S. copyright site at   www.copyright.gov   or   at   Cornell   University's   site   at www4.law.cornell.edu/uscode/17/ch1.html.

5.   Attorney Richard Hammar's *The Church Guide to Copyright Law* (Matthews, N.C.: Christian Ministry Resources, 2001) provides specific guidance for church leaders wishing to know more about their legal obligations and rights. The "narrow exception" of the religious services exemption is discussed on page 89 in his book.

6.   From the Nonlegislative Report of the Subcommittee on Courts and Intellectual Property, Committee on the Judiciary, U.S. House of Representatives, *Fair Use Guidelines for Educational Multimedia*, prepared by Carlos Moorhead and Patricia Schroeder, July 17, 1996. The text may be found at Penn State's Web site at www.libraries.psu.edu/mtss/fairuse/guidelinedoc.html.

7.   Ibid.

8.   ASCAP's Web site offers licensing information and their view of the church worship exemption at www.ascap.com/licensing/licensingfaq.html.

9.   BMI emailed me on April 13, 1999 to say that "The Copyright Law makes provisions for the exemption of churches for public 'performance of music in the course of religious services at a place of worship . . .'" Their Web site is found at www.bmi.com.

10. From *Fair Use Guidelines for Educational Multimedia*.

11. Thanks to Teri Dary for providing this listing of equipment needed for multimedia worship.

12. NEC Technologies, in an advertisement flyer, "Sense-sational Presentations." The company Web site is at www.nectech.com.

Appendix A. Frequently Asked Questions

1.   These guidelines are available at a number of Web sites. The one I found most helpful, because it shows original documents associated with

fair use guidelines, is at the Penn State University Web site, www.libraries.psu.edu/mtss/fairuse/guidelinedoc.html.

2.   These additional guidelines are available at www.copyright.gov and may be accessed by typing in a search box, "guidelines for off-air recording" and then clicking on "Circular 21," "Circular United States Copyright Office 21 Reproduction of Copyrighted Works by Educators and Librarians." Click on "Circular 21" and you will be taken to the "Guidelines for Off-air Recording of Broadcast Programming for Educational Purposes" provided as excerpts from the House Report on piracy and counterfeiting amendments (H.R. 97-495, pp. 8–9).

Appendix B. A Service of Dedication for a Sanctuary Projection Screen

1.   I recommend stanza 3 of "For the Beauty of the Earth." The quoted stanza is by Folliott S. Pierpoint, as found in *The Pilgrim Hymnal* (New York: The Pilgrim Press, 1931, renewed 1986), no. 366. This third stanza of the hymn can remind us that what we see and hear through multimedia worship may bring us delightful thoughts and feelings while helping us to praise God.

Books

Babin, Pierre. *The New Era in Religious Communication*. Minneapolis: Fortress Press, 1991.

Babin describes in great detail how the 16th-century church leapt into print technology to promote its messages, and how that technology helped fuel the Protestant Reformation. Yet today's church has been slow to respond to the possibilities for applying electronic technology to education and worship. He defines an "alphabetical orientation" that is distinct from an "electronic media orientation," and how the church must respond to a new generation that is much more media oriented than they are print oriented.

Beaudoin, Tom. *Virtual Faith: The Irreverent Spiritual Quest of Generation X*. San Francisco: Jossey-Bass, 1998.

Affirming that there are religious themes in popular culture, the author recommends churches take popular culture seriously. Generation X is formed by popular culture as a primary source of meaning and all attempts to address spirituality must be interpreted and understood through that culture. Noting that God talk is prevalent in our culture, the book reminds us of the spiritual material waiting to be uncovered in the popular media of our time.

Beckett, Wendy, C.S.J. *A Child's Book of Prayer in Art*. New York: Dorling Kindersley Publishing, Inc., 1995.

"Looking at art is one way of listening to God," writes Sister Wendy Beckett. This book offers a simple way for children of all ages to look at great art and understand it with the eyes of faith. Although the book is written for children, it offers a quick way for adults with a childlike understanding of art to learn how to interpret art for the worship setting.

130 Silver Screen, Sacred Story

Brueggemann, Walter. *Texts Under Negotiation: The Bible and Postmodern Imagination.* Minneapolis: Fortress Press, 1993.

Brueggemann defines our postmodern era and what that means for the church. He thinks we will most effectively communicate biblical themes by stimulating the imagination, and finding new ways to bring the stories to life in our time and place. While he does not speak about using electronic media in worship, he says that when we open up biblical story to a fresh, new hearing and viewing, we join in a "counterimagination of the world."

Collins, James C., and Jerry I. Porras. *Built to Last: Successful Habits of Visionary Companies.* New York: HarperBusiness, 1994.

"Companies that enjoy enduring success have core values and a core purpose that remain fixed while business strategies and practices endlessly adapt to a changing world." Replace the word church for words like company and business, and you have a guide for understanding how to navigate change through an organization. The writers tell us that enduring organizations preserve their core values "while stimulating progress." This material, adapted into a congregational setting, can help church leaders identify the core values of their church and align changes with those values. The identification and planning process they suggest to leaders is streamlined, quick, and easy. A shorter version of their thesis, "Building Your Company's Vision," may be found in the September–October 1996 issue of the *Harvard Business Review.*

Collins, Jim. *Good to Great: Why Some Companies Make the Leap . . . and Others Don't.* New York: HarperBusiness, 2001.

This is an excellent study about what distinguishes great organizations from mediocre ones. Using plenty of examples from actual companies, Collins identifies the kind of leadership required for great organizations, the central energy source that brings about the greatest results, and the unstoppable power of gradual change. Is your church a great church or is it on the "doom loop?" Read this book to learn what you as a leader need to do about it, and what to stop doing. The good news: greatness in our organizations requires that leaders work smart while doing less.

Cox, Harvey. *The Seduction of the Spirit.* New York: Simon and Schuster, 1973.

Thirty years after it was written, this book is a reminder that Protestantism continues to emphasize words over images and that the time is long overdue for us to "redress the balance" and recover the power of image in worship.

Crowley-Horak, Eileen. "Testing the Fruits: Liturgical Aesthetics as Applied to Liturgical Media Art," Dissertation (Unpublished). New York: Union Theological Seminary, 2002.

    The dissertation features a history of media art in U.S. churches, definitions of "liturgical media art," interviews with clergy and lay leaders using media art in worship, and addresses the place of beauty (aesthetics) in mediated worship. Calling technology secondary to liturgy, Crowley-Horak explains that "Forming and reinforcing relationships with God, the world, and each other is the unexpected fruit of this art-and-technology hybrid."

Dyer, Scott, and Nancy Beach. *The Source: Resource Guide for Using Creative Arts in Church Services*. Grand Rapids, Mich.: Zondervan Publishing House, 1996.

    This book suggests worship themes and message titles, along with song, film clip, and drama suggestions to illustrate the themes. Not only do the authors give a number of film clip suggestions, but they also provide the location of the recommended clip in the film by including the start and finish time of the scene.

Easum, William. *Dancing with Dinosaurs*. Nashville: Abingdon Press, 1993.

    Read anything you can find by Bill Easum. This is just one of his many resources available in print and online. He advocates that churches become culturally relevant and lay-directed. Worship must become indigenous; that is, responsive to the music and viewing habits of unique congregations. He encourages clergy and laity to find direction from the book of Acts and "make disciples" while claiming the new mission field to be the world at our doorstep.

Fields, Doug, and Eddie James. *Videos That Teach*. El Cajon, Calif.: Youth Specialties Books, 1999.

    Indexed by movie title, topic, and scripture, this book offers a synopsis of each film, the location of the video clip, its relationship to scripture and topic, and questions for discussion. It is a good book to have when trying to locate film clips related to your scriptural or topical themes.

Friedman, Edwin H. *Generation to Generation: Family Process in Church and Synagogue.* New York: The Guilford Press, 1985.

The section on self-differentiated leadership is most useful as leaders claim a vision for using visuals in worship. Leaders staying on a growing, learning edge will naturally share that excitement with their congregations, and bring them along on the journey. The family systems theory information will also come in handy once your teams start working together. Understanding family system dynamics in relationship to congregations may help resolve communication dysfunctions that emerge as your team works together.

Hammar, Richard R. *The Church Guide to Copyright Law.* Matthews, N.C.: Christian Ministry Resources, 2001.

This guide offers information for those who want clarification about copyright law in relationship to typical church situations. While very thorough, this edition of the text, first written in 1988, still lacks any clear direction about the use of multimedia resources in the worship setting. We can only hope that such resources will appear as more churches begin to use more media in worship.

Lindvall, Terry. *The Silents of God: Selected Issues and Documents in Silent American Film and Religion 1908–1925.* Lanham, Md.: Scarecrow Press, Inc. 2001.

Incredibly, ministers were incorporating multimedia in their worship and teaching services way back in 1909. Congregational ministers were writing how-to manuals for other churches interested in "The Religious Possibilities of the Motion Picture" and recommended, "let the scripture lesson be illustrated with a film exhibiting the very incident narrated by the Bible." Those media pioneers offered advice for "how to preach by motion pictures." Once again we learn how our generation is not the first to pioneer with technology. Lindvall and his students have uncovered a treasury of primary documents about the history of using multimedia in worship.

Malone, Peter, and Rose Pacatte. *Lights, Camera . . . Faith!* Boston: Pauline Books and Media, 2001.

These authors have provided a lectionary-based movie scene guide. Three volumes are based on years A, B, and C of the lectionary. They provide a film recommendation for one of the lectionary texts of the week, a synopsis of the film, a "dialogue with the Gospel," key scenes and themes, a reflection or conversation starter, and a prayer. Their books are thorough and provide a thoughtful teaching and learning resource.

Mucciolo, Tom, and Rich Mucciolo. *Purpose, Movement, Color: A Strategy for Effective Presentations.* New York: MediaNet, Inc. 1994.

Before any of us stands in front of a screen to present a computer-enhanced message, we should read this short book. Using research on the impact of color and shape on the human mind, speaker placement in relationship to screen, and the power of purposeful communication, the writers give the basics for electronic presentations.

Ong, Walter. *Orality and Literacy: The Technologizing of the Word.* London and New York: Methuen, 1982.

Ong's work is good reading for those looking for a deeper theoretical discussion about the relationship between oral culture, print culture, and the "secondary orality" emerging through electronic culture. Likening today's electronic culture as more akin to that of oral, nonliterate cultures, Ong stimulates thinking about the similarities of Jesus' parable or oral culture to the storytelling function of today's electronic media.

Phillips, Roy D. *Letting Go: Transforming Congregations for Ministry.* Bethesda, Md.: The Alban Institute, 1999.

This book provides a way of thinking about leadership roles among clergy and laity, and how it is so important for clergy to "get out of the way" so that gifted leaders can emerge within our congregations. Team-oriented leadership where teams take responsibility for what they do is a clear result of the transformation possible as clergy and laity rethink how they fulfill their common mission.

Sample, Tex. *The Spectacle of Worship in a Wired World: Electronic Culture and the Gathered People of God.* Nashville: Abingdon Press, 1998.

Tex Sample advocates designing worship that uses the music and imagery of electronic culture to communicate the Gospel through "the construction of an experience." He has been advocating "media-enhanced worship" and culturally relevant worship for a long time. "Incarnation is how we understand our picture in terms of God's greater picture."

Schlain, Leonard. *The Alphabet Versus the Goddess: The Conflict Between Word and Image*. New York: Viking Press, 1998.

The author is a brain surgeon who applies his knowledge of the human brain to his theory that writing culture and the alphabet reduced the human imagination, and that by returning images to our life we will increase "awareness of beauty." It is an interesting look at how both word and image have great power, and to emphasize one at the expense of the other is to reduce our mental and cultural options.

Sweet, Leonard. *Postmodern Pilgrims: First Century Passion for the 21st Century World*. Nashville: Broadman and Holman Publishers, 2000.

Sweet will rearrange your thinking about the present communication situation. In this book, he develops what he calls the EPIC model "of doing church that is biblically absolute but culturally relative: Experiential, Participatory, Image-driven, Connected." Success is measured by "creativity and imagination." His books affirm efforts to develop multimedia worship, providing us with a practical and biblical foundation.

Teilhard de Chardin, Pierre. *The Divine Milieu*. New York: Harper and Row, 1960.

Teilhard's gift was merging his scientific training with his calling as a priest. As such, he writes this mystical book about the relationship of the world to God, and how all life is lived within a divine milieu, at once embracing matter and being sparked by divinity. His musings remind us of the theological meanings embedded in all of life.

Tillich, Paul. *Theology of Culture*. New York: Oxford University Press, 1964.

Tillich long advocated the use of the arts in worship, and identified how church and culture are inextricably woven together. "In poetry, in visual art, and in music, levels of reality are opened up which can be opened up in no other way." Opened to these new experiences, the soul itself gains a deeper interiority. His discussion about the role of religious symbol in worship is a reminder of the power of visuals in worship.

Wheatley, Margaret J. *Leadership and the New Science*. San Francisco: Berrett-Koehler Publishers, Inc., 1994.

This book is extremely useful for understanding new ways of thinking about leadership and organizations from the perspective of quantum science.

Old models of the Industrial Age, which presume closed systems (like motors) and inherent deterioration of structures (like death), are giving way to new models based on the new science. She talks of nonmaterial "fields" like information (and prayer), that, when shared throughout an organization, refresh and renew the system. Systems organized around strong cores of meaning called "strange attractors" become resilient as they move into the future. Important chapters include "The Creative Energy of the Universe—Information" and "Change, Stability, and Renewal: The Paradoxes of Self-Organizing Systems."

White, Susan J. *Christian Worship and Technological Change.* Nashville: Abingdon Press, 1994.

This book is for those unsure about whether it is appropriate to use technology in worship. White reminds us that the church has always been incorporating technology into its life. Clocks, the printing press, and learning how to make unfermented grape juice are but three examples of how the church has been shaped by, and shapes with, technology. She offers a model for embracing technology in religious communities.

Whitehead, James D., and Evelyn Eaton Whitehead. *The Promise of Partnership: A Model for Collaborative Ministry.* San Francisco: HarperSanFrancisco, 1991.

Churches must address issues of leadership, partnership, and power if they are to fully develop their mission. Power sharing within the church helps us define who we are as a people of God. "We are meant to play together in the bewildering but creative drama of Christian life."

Woods, C. Jeff. *Congregational Megatrends.* Bethesda, Md.: The Alban Institute, 1996.

Our congregation's long-range planning team read this book as they began to envision a future for their church. They studied several of Woods's trends, such as the move to hands-on mission, gifted leadership, holographic programming, and primary planning, as they considered what a new, innovative worship experience might be like.

Internet Resources

Search engines such as Google (www.google.com) and Alta Vista (www.altavista.com) allow users to conduct a search of images found on the Internet. Click on the "Image" link above the navigation textbox on these Web sites to access this specialized search engine. Enter keywords and phrases that describe the type of imagery desired. Results are provided in the form of thumbnail images, which are linked to the Web site containing the full-sized images. Other image search engines include:

www.ditto.com
www.search-engine-index.co.uk
www.powerpointbackgrounds.com (downloadable backgrounds for PowerPoint)

Art Resources

www.artchive.com. A collection of art masterpieces with high quality images available for free download for educational purposes (suggestion: support this site by becoming a donor).
www.wsu.edu/~dee/ An excellent site that provides background information on world art.
www.message.sk. A great site for some interesting high-quality abstract art.

Songs

www.members.tripod.com/~ylime_/ An interesting collection of song lyrics.
www.song1.com. Search for lyrics, artists, titles of songs, or by lyric phrase, name, or song title.
www.lyrics.com. A miscellaneous collection of song lyrics.

Movie Reviews

www.hollywoodjesus.com. Movie reviews with an eye toward religious meanings and symbolism.

www.textweek.com. Provides a scripture study organized by scripture and theme, integrated with a movie and art concordance.

www.mrqe.com. A movie review search engine, allowing you to browse through a variety of reviews about your choice of movies, sorted by various sites, newspapers, and magazines. Search by title or degree of popularity.

www.screenit.com. Offers reviews of music and movies, providing information geared toward parents with respect to content, which includes violence, alcohol and drugs, sex, profanity, and a variety of other issues.

Multimedia Worship Resources

www.worshipmedia.com. This is my own site, and it offers film clip and song suggestions for illustrating various scriptural themes, as well as a way to connect with other people using multimedia in worship.

Welcome to the work of Alban Institute...
the leading publisher and congregational resource organization for clergy and laity today.

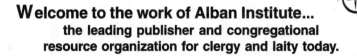

Your purchase of this book means you have an interest in the kinds of information, research, consulting, networking opportunities and educational seminars that Alban Institute produces and provides. We are a non-denominational, non-profit 25-year-old membership organization dedicated to providing practical and useful support to religious congregations and those who participate in and lead them.

Alban is acknowledged as a pioneer in learning and teaching on *Conflict Management *Faith and Money *Congregational Growth and Change *Leadership Development *Mission and Planning *Clergy Recruitment and Training *Clergy Support, Self-Care and Transition *Spirituality and Faith Development *Congregational Security.

Our membership is comprised of over 8,000 clergy, lay leaders, congregations and institutions who benefit from:
  ❖ 15% discount on hundreds of Alban books
  ❖ $50 per-course tuition discount on education seminars
  ❖ Subscription to *Congregations*, the Alban journal (a $30 value)
  ❖ Access to Alban research and (soon) the "Members-Only" archival section of our web site www.alban.org

For more information on Alban membership or to be added to our catalog mailing list, call 1-800-486-1318, ext.243 or return this form.

Name and Title: _____

Congregation/Organization: _____

Address: _____

City: _____ Tel.: _____

State: _____ Zip: _____ Email: _____

BKIN

The Alban Institute
Attn: Membership Dept.
7315 Wisconsin Avenue
Suite 1250 West
Bethesda, MD 20814-3211